To

Shambhavi and Aishwary

……..In journey towards infinity and

immortality……..

From

Mummy and Papa

Forewords

As a product is positioned and pushed, it makes a road entry into market, but a brand is something which enters into mind and heart of people and remains there for generations. There is no single way it happens, but there are innumerable ways of it happening. This book is about what are the various ways to build a brand. The book also analyses macro level factors as well as micro level factors, which are responsible in making of a brand in its existing form and stature. While macro types of branding strategies discussed in the book have roots in previous academic work, micro factors of branding strategies emanates from the practice in

the industry as understood by the author. By understanding these micro and macro factors and branding matrix analysis, a brand manager has a forceful tool in his hands to fortify an existing brand or to create a new brand.

I am thankful to CreateSpace for making this book possible. Any criticism, feedback and suggestion about the book are most welcome.

Author

Contents

Part 1. Brand Introduction

Part 2. Macro Branding Strategies

Part 3. Micro Branding Strategies

Part 4. Branding Matrix Analysis

Part 5. Glossary

Self published

Author : Aravind Kumar Chaturvedi

vedic4marketing@gmail.com

Printed by CreateSpace

Price US$9.50

Available at www.Amazon.com and other retail stores

Spectrum of Branding Strategy

Part1

Brand Introduction

Introduction

A Brand, intrinsically is image and feeling of an entity in mind and heart of people. Two brands are differentiated by what people opine about them. Extrinsically, a Brand is a word collection or design or an image or other feature that represents an organization or product in the memory of the people. Brands are used in business for effective communication and establishing a long lasting relationship between owner of the brand, people and customers.

A brand essentially, is a promise from a corporate to its customers about benefits, features and usefulness they can expect from products as well as emotional benefits. From customers perspective, a brand is taken as guaranteed satisfaction from purchase of a product. The customer is not certain about level of satisfaction, he would achieve from purchase of same product but unbranded. Thus brand is taken as assurance of value, when purchasing a product. This means that consumers buy brand rather than product.

A brand comes into being with attributes associated with it as per wish of the corporate. A corporate may wish to label its brand "Pollution free". Thus pollution free becomes one attribute of the brand. Similarly corporate may wish to associate the brand with few more labels, which become attributes of the brand. But a customer is lured not just by attributes alone resulting into purchase of the product, then benefits of the brand must also be highlighted to the customer. Here in this case benefit of having a safe environment for next generations could be highlighted as benefit of the brand, when a customer subscribe to it. Also a corporate may associate it with certain value to which it is committed, so as to get response from all those, who believe in the same value. Thus a corporate identifies it's brand in perspectives of attributes, benefits and values. There are at least two perspectives, a consumer views a brand along, psychological and experiential. Psychologically a brand is symbolic to specific thoughts, feelings, images, belief and attitudes. Experiential perspective is built by experience when customer comes into contact of the brand. It is impression about brand qualities which are unique and not available in other brands.

Brands are classified into many types by authors and academicians. Some of the types of brands identified are

1. Attitude Brands : when a brand is promoted based on feeling rather than physical characteristics of a product, it is called attitude brand. The feeling may be sense of freedom or sense of strength etc.

2. **Symbolic Brands** : What attitude brands are to product, symbolic brands are same to a service. Symbolic brands are used for service providing organizations such as banks cargo and courier, airlines and telecom companies.

   Branding is pitched with emotional aspect of service such as sense of security, round the clock service etc. to attract and retain customers.

3. **Functional Brands** : Many products and services have more powerful and attractive physical or functional characteristics compared to any feeling and emotional aspects of the products and services. This could be best price, best performance or unique feature not available in others. When brand is created based on physical and functional aspect of a product or service, it is called functional brand.

4. **Individual Brands** : Sometimes an organization opt to name each product or service offered, a separate brand name. These brands might compete with each other in the market for example flavors of deodorants, soft drinks or cosmetics. Such brands are called individual brands.

5. **Own Brands** : The brands that are named after retailers name are called own brands. Large retail chains and superstores use own brands.

6. **Product Brand :** Product brands are brands that are affiliated to a tangible product, a motorcycle, a biscuit or a toothpaste. Product brands comprise of a specific product or a range of product in same product category.

7. **Service Brand :** Business activities have shifted from tangible product manufacturing to complete solution and intangible service. Term service brand is used in case of organizations and activities involving service. Service brands are focused on "what is done", "when and who does it" etc.

8. **Concept Brand :** when a concept is branded instead of a product or service, the brand is called concept brand. The concept could be "save earth", or "save girl child" etc.

9. **Organization Brand :** When organization name is used to brand its all products and services, the brand is termed organization brand. Organization brand is thus created as sum of all offered products and all offered services. When organization is a corporate, the brand is treated as a corporate brand.

10. **Personal Brand :** Personal brand is focused on few individuals. A personal brand may be focused on one celebrity, for example a beautician or may be focused on a group, for example a pop group.

11. Sensory Brands : Brands which seduce public by senses such as vision, color, sound , odor or touch are classified as sensory brands.

12. Event Brand :Events like car race or Rock can also be characterized as brands.

13. Geographic Brand : Areas can be characterized based on certain facilities and hence centers or cities can also be brands. When area chosen to brand and mange is a nation, the brand is termed as nation brand

Branding process involves two facets,

1. Physiological process

2. Psychological process

1. Physiological process

A brand exists in a physical form. Physiological processes involve in branding are designing a brand name, trademark, logo or symbol in such a way that the brand and its mapping in any of these forms relate to each other effectively. Physiological processes are more of an art and legal activity, rather than marketing activity.

Physical elements of a brand are,

Name : Brand name is a word or collection of words used to identify a brand. Brand name is written or spoken linguistic element of a Product and is a type of trade mark. A trade mark can be protected by trademark registration. After legal registration a trademark is called registered trademark and can not be used by others.

Logo : A logo is visual trade mark which identify a brand.

Tagline : A line appended to the visual part of the brand.

Besides name, logo and tagline a Brand may opt to have physical elements like graphics, shapes, color and sound etc.

2. Psychological process

An image, feeling and value of a brand remains in the mind of people. The brand image is more vivid in the mind of existing users and possible customers. Thus a brand exists in psychological form, which is more important than its physiological form for marketing purpose.

To create a brand, the image, feeling and value of the new brand has to be carved in the memory of targeted customers by efforts of the owner of the brand, which starts with

1. Creating an unique product or service or concept bundled with unmatched usefulness to people in a unique way, which no other competitors offer.

2. Ensuring that promised usefulness is integral to the product and is really delivered.

3. Finally, communication to the market that promises are affirmatively delivered.

A brand can not sustain without brand communication. Presently integrated marketing communications (IMC) are being practiced to communicate brand identity. There are five components of the IMC, advertising, sales promotion, direct marketing, personal selling and public relations. Brands intended message is communicated through IMC. Effective communication results, if customers perceive exactly the intended message.

Spectrum of Branding Strategy

Part2

Macro Branding Strategies

Contents

Macro Branding Strategies

1. Individual Branding Strategy
2. Multi Product Branding Strategy
3. Multi Branding Strategy
4. Sub Branding Strategy
5. Co-Branding Strategy
6. Reseller Branding Strategy
7. Mixed Branding Strategy
8. Private Branding Strategy
9. No-Brand Branding Strategy
10. Derived Branding Strategy

1. Individual Branding Strategy

Individual branding strategy is practice, wherein a brand name is given to each products of the company in a single product segment. Often the company own several brands in the same product segment and these products compete with each other. Soaps and detergents are one of the product segment in which the individual branding strategy is very commonplace.

Hindustan Unilever has applied this strategy in detergent segment. It has several brands in detergent segment such as Surf excel, Active wheel, Sunlight and Rin. These brands compete not only with the brands of other companies such as Ariel and Tide of Proctor and Gamble but also among themselves.

Company: Hindustan Unilever	Product : Detergent	Brands: Surf Excel Active Wheel Sunlight Rin

This strategy is most suitable where consumer base is very large in number and there are many possible sizes, flavors and tastes of the product. The loyalty of customers towards the brand is fluctuating and there are many brands present in the market. The company therefore presents many brand options to the consumers among its own brands, so as not to loose business to brands of some other company.

Initially there is equilibrium among the brands in the market. The war begins when a player breaks the equilibrium by announcing a big leap in feature, cost or quality of its existing brand or by launch of a new brand. This event creates a disequilibrium in the market and triggers many reactions from players in the market. One of the reaction is, launch of a new brand besides an existing brand. This leads to strategy of many brands in one product segment.

The obvious advantage of this strategy is, when a customer changes his loyalty from a brand, it likely that he switches to a brand owned by the company itself.

2. Multi Product Branding Strategy

Multi product branding strategy is practice of marketing products of many segments under one brand name. Though products are from many segments, essentially the targeted market is same.

Consumer goods company Hindustan Unilever (HUL) markets products in various segments under one brand Dove. Several segment touched are Dove bar and skin care, Dove anti perspirent, Dove hair care and Dove lotions and cream etc. All products are related to personal care. Thus essentially most of the consumers need the entire range of the products offered.

Brand : Dove	Dove Bar and Skin care
	Dove Hair care
	Dove Anti perspirent
	Dove Lotion and Cream

Macro Branding Strategies

Multi Product Branding may be sub classified into

1. Corporate Branding
2. Family Branding
3. Umbrella Branding

When corporate name is promoted as brand name for marketing many products across several product segments, the multi product branding strategy is called corporate branding. Reliance and Apple are some corporate brands. Reliance brand is used across many product segments such as petrol pumps, Retail chain and mobile services. Similarly Apple brand is used to promote computers and mobile.

Corporate : Reliance	Reliance Petroleum Retail
	Reliance Stores
	Reliance Mobile service
	Reliance Textiles

Spectrum of Branding Strategy

When family name is chosen as brand name to promote many products, the multi product branding strategy is called family branding. TATA name brand is one such example. TATA family brand is used to promote tea, coffee, salt and steel etc. products extensively in India and abroad.

Family : TATA	TATA Salt
	TATA Tea
	TATA Coffee
	TATA Motors

When a brand name is used to promote several products across multiple product segments, the branding strategy is called umbrella branding strategy. The brand name acts as umbrella name for promoting the products.

Macro Branding Strategies

Cadbury is an example of umbrella brand, which spreads across chocolates, confectionary, beverages and desserts.

Brand : Cadbury	Brands :
Segments :	Dairy Milk
	Dairy Milk fruit & nut
Chocolates	Dairy Milk Caramel
Confectionary	Eclairs
Desserts	Crunchie
Beverages	Shots
	Snack
	Snow Flake
	Cream egg
	Fingers
	Flake
	Brunch
	Dairy Milk silk
	Dairy Milk bliss
	Dairy Milk silk oreo

3. Multi Branding Strategy

Multi branding strategy emphasizes on promoting a brand for each product and maintains a long list of brands across many product segments. Consumer goods and pharmaceutical multinational companies often use multi branding strategy. Hindustan Unilever owns brands such as Lipton, Surf, Lux, Cornetto, Ponds, Sunsilk, Axe, Vaseline and Bru to name a few, Nestle owns brands such as Nescafe, Maggie, Nesvita, Crunch, Cerelac etc. and Pfizer owns brands such as Lipitor, Lyrica, Zithromax and Diflucan etc.

Company: Hindustan Unilever	Brands	Product segment
	Lipton	Tea
	Surf	Detergent
	Lux	Soap
	Cornetto	Ice Cream
	Ponds	Cold cream
	Sunsilk	Shampoo
	Axe	Deodorant
	Vaseline	Skin care
	Bru	Instant coffee

Macro Branding Strategies

The multi branding strategy is costly because advertising and promotion cost of each brand has to be incurred. But this cost is balanced by the fact that non success of one brand does not impact adversely the performance of the other brands.

Multi Branding also maintains the balance sheet when few products are losing demand with diversified presence. It is therefore helpful in steady and balanced growth of a large corporate.

Company: Pfizer	Brands	Product segment
	Lipitor	Blood Cholesterol control
	Lyrica	Neuropathic
	Zithromax	Antibiotic
	Diflucan	Antifungal
	Cerebra	Antifungal

4. Sub Branding Strategy

Sub branding strategy is used to introduce new products in the existing product class, which targets a different market segment.

Sub brands are created under a brand to target specific market segments. Maruti automobile has car sub brands like Maruti Alto, Maruti Wagon R, Maruti dezire, Maruti Boleno and Maruti Swift etc. Each sub brand is intended for a different market segment in the same product class. Here Alto, Dezire, Boleno and Swift are sub brands of maruti car.

| Brand: Maruti | Sub Brands: Alto, Swift, Boleno, Dezire |

Sub branding is different from multi product branding in the way, that it is restricted in one product segment where as multi product branding strategies like corporate, family or umbrella branding is not restricted to one product segment and which are rather diversified in many product segments.

A market is a dynamic entity. It's segmentation is a continuous process, in which some new segments are created and some existing segments vanish. Sub branding is response to this market segment dynamism. As soon as a new market segment comes into being, a sub brand must be launched to tap the new segment in order to fortify the brand.

Launch of product variants may not be truly called sub branding. Android, a software for touch screen interaction by Google has products Android TV, Android Auto and Android Wear meant respectively for touch screen enabled televisions, automobiles and wrist watches. These can not be called sub brands of android in true sense because they are means to port same functionality on different devices. Sub branding involves with using different technologies, adding new features, functions and usefulness rather than just porting same function to some other platform.

Spectrum of Branding Strategy

Cadbury is a good example of sub brands too, with sub brands like Dairy Milk fruit & nut, Dairy Milk caramel and Dairy Milk Silk etc. under brand Dairy Milk.

Corporate : Cadbury Segment : Chocolate Brand : Dairy Milk	Sub Brands of Dairy Milk Dairy Milk Fruit & nut Dairy Milk Caramel Dairy Milk Silk Dairy Milk Bliss Dairy Milk silk Oreo

5. Co-Branding Strategy

Co-brands are created by combining two brands in order to create a new synergy. Hero-Honda or Maruti-Suzuki or Tata-Tetly are all co-brands.

The need of a co-brand is felt when a Brand can not compete alone, with other competitor brands present. It is perceived that with help of another foreign brand, an advantage over other brands can be achieved. In this situation two brands may agree to create a co-brand, which will benefit both of them. Competition alone is not the only need of creating a co-brand. Every brand has a specific strength. A co-brand unites the strengths of two brands in one product. An example of co-brand is brand Ashok Leyland in commercial vehicles. This brand is result of combination of two brands, Ashok Motors of Chennai, India and Leyland Motors of England. Ashok Motors was intended to assemble and distribute cars and thus had strength in car segment. But seeing the demand for commercial vehicles in India then, they ventured with Leyland Motors of England, which was a major english commercial vehicle manufacturer with substantial strength in commercial vehicle segment. This co-venturing as old as dated 1954, resulted into a strong co-Brand Ashok Leyland in commercial vehicle segment and is being marketed world wide today.

Spectrum of Branding Strategy

1948		1954
Brand : Ashok Motors, India	+	Brand : Leyland Motors, England
Strength :		Strength :
Distribution and manufacture of cars in India		Distribution and manufacture of commercial vehicles in England

=

Co-Brand : Ashok Leyland
Reach : Global
Segment : commercial vehicles

A Co-Brand may be build within the corporate or organization. An example is brand Lakme Lever. The brand Lakme is owned by Hindustan Lever itself. The corporate has decided to venture into beauty care segment with brand name Lakme Lever. The reason behind this may be fact that Lakme is a well known Brand in beauty products and Hindustan Unilever is a well known corporate brand with proven management ability. This gives a good synergy to start a beauty care chain under a co-Brand Lakme Lever by combining beauty Brand Lakme and corporate Brand Hindustan Unilever.

```
┌─────────────────────────┐         ┌─────────────────────────┐
│ Brand : Lakme           │         │ Brand : Hindustan Unilever│
│                         │         │ Strength :              │
│ Strength :              │    +    │                         │
│ Well known Beauty       │         │ Largest FMCG Corporate  │
│ Product Brand           │         │ Brand with multi brands │
└─────────────────────────┘         └─────────────────────────┘

                            =

              ┌─────────────────────────────┐
              │ Co-Brand : Lakme Lever      │
              │                             │
              │ Product : Lakme Beauty      │
              │           Salon Chain       │
              └─────────────────────────────┘
```

Since, Lakme brand is owned by Hindustan Unilever itself and therefore, this is one example of co-Branding within organization.

Joint ventures are not synonymous to co-branding, but many often they result in a successful co-brand. In emerging economies in want of funds, joint ventures are formed with multinational companies. It gives multinationals a new geography to expand their business. TATA DoCoMo, IFFCO Tokyo, Bharti Axa, HDFC Standard, Future Generali, ICICI Prudential are such example in Indian context. The success of joint venture depends on affinity and synergy between the partner companies as well as business acumen. A successful joint venture definitely results into a strong co-brands.

Cadbury co-brands chocolates box with a packaging company brand roses as Cadbury roses.

6. Reseller Branding Strategy

Over time many stores which directly sell the products have become a symbol of quality and reliability. Retail chains which often run stores at multiple locations across cities have become brand in itself. Walmart may be cited as an example of retail brand. Many manufacturers supply their products to the superstores, which resell the products under superstore's brand name. This branding strategy is called reseller branding strategy or store branding strategy. The advantage to manufacturer under this branding strategy is that they can save a lot of expenditures, which would have been spent on advertising and branding exercise on account of building a reliable brand. This reduces the cost of products. On the other side, the advantage to the selling superstore is that it can source a good quality product at a lower price. Besides Walmart, there are several other superstore chains like Sears, Kroger, Tesco and Carrefour etc.

Reseller Branding strategy include manufacture to supply specialized retail chain stores dedicated to a particular product segments. Besides departmental stores, There are retail chain stores meant for electronic goods, furniture or jewelry and clothing etc.

7. Mixed Branding Strategy

Mix brands are created by combining a manufacturer brand and a reseller brand. Mix branding strategy is adopted by manufacturers, when entering a new territory or when they manufacture across various product categories. For example, a home appliance maker like Whirlpool and Samsung, if wish to enter a foreign market, it will be best suited for them to create a mix brand with a retail brand in the foreign country. Another need of a mix brand arise when a manufacturer is diversified in segments like cosmetics, skin care and herbal beauty care, it may organize its sales strategy to create a mix brand for its skin care with a retail brand and sell other products under own brand. This is an easy way to reach another market segment which does not have good affinity to itself. Mixed brands are different from co-brands in the way that co-brands are created by combination of two manufacturer brands, while in mix brand one partner is a reseller.

| De Beers (Diamond manufacturer brand) | + | Asmi (reseller brand owned by Gitanjali gems) |

=

| De Beers Asmi (Diamond jewellery mix brand) |

The difference in making of a mix brand and co-brand is explained below.

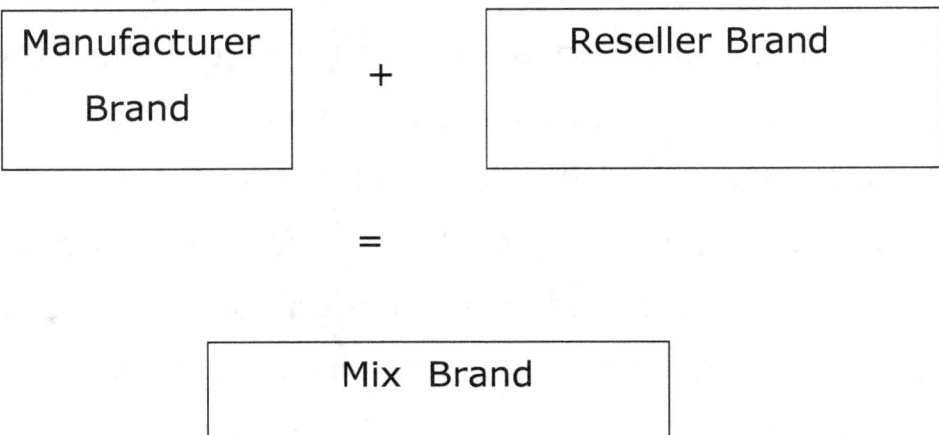

A mix brand is created by combining a manufacturer brand with a reseller brand and a co-brand is created by combining two manufacturer brands.

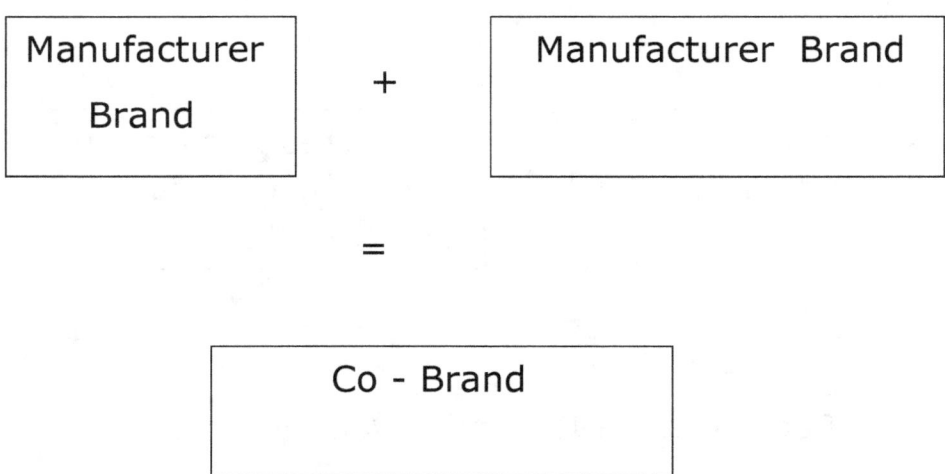

8. Private Branding Strategy

Private branding strategy involves product manufactured by one company is offered for sale under brand name of another company. This branding is under practice over a number of industries such as cosmetics, home appliances, electronic goods, food and beverages and apparel. These are commonly placed against established brands as a low cost substitute, though there is change in this viewpoint and private labels are now being placed as premium products also. Videocon of India has made Hyundai durable range of products as its private label brand. The private branding strategy differs from reseller brands in that the selling company is not just a reseller or store brand but an integrated company from manufacturing to distribution.

9. No-Brand Branding Strategy

The business exists in two class organized and unorganized. It is general tendency that business in unorganized sector tends to go into organized sector over time. One example is retail stores. Presently, many big corporates have entered into this business, which was once in hands of small shops owned by individuals. People visit retail chains on occasion, as well as to small shops to purchase.

No-branding is reverse process in which, organized sector imitate to be at par with unorganized sector to tap business in this class. In general, goods bought from a branded store is a taken as granted to possess a good quality at a little high cost. If dominating factor for a buyer is quality, he goes to branded product from large store, but if cost is dominating factor he is likely to go to a reasonable price shop to get an unbranded product, but with reasonable quality at a low price. Under no-branding strategy, the manufacturer saves entire campaigning and advertising cost. More attention is given to cost control of the product, for its wider acceptability. Most of the manufacturing outsourcing companies fall under no-brand branding strategy, since these companies do not sell under their own label or brand. Generic branding is also no brand branding.

10. Derived Branding Strategy

Derived branding strategy depends upon component brands. Several Personal computer manufacturers brand their products based upon names of Intel or AMD, depending upon chips used in the manufactured computer. The chip is the component part of a computer. Intel or AMD are component brands in this case. The component brands are technically so sound and well accepted by the market and customers that a manufacturer is more proud and confident of the component brand rather than its own brand.

Derived branding becomes important when components or ingredients brand is well established in market with a seal of reliability and quality. In many cases component brand monopolize the market and is most essential part of the product. Importance of ingredient or component can be easily highlighted by engines of airplanes, which are the most crucial and sophisticated component of an airplane. General Electric GEnx and Rolls Royce Trent1000 aviation engines can be cited as two ingredient brands of which, Boeing also is proud of.

Macro Branding Strategies

Spectrum of Branding Strategy

Part 3

Micro Branding Strategies

In previous chapter, several branding strategies were illustrated. All those branding strategies, whether Individual branding, Multi product branding, Sub branding, Private branding or Co-branding, are part of a broader approach to branding strategy. For this reason those branding strategies were classified as Macro Branding Strategies. These strategies are formulated mostly at the corporate and brand level, neglecting fundamental forces and factors, which drive the product, market and consumer.

There are several fundamental aspects of branding strategies, which are decisive in order to finalize whether to go for Co-branding or Sub branding, whether to opt for Individual branding or Multi product branding. There are grass root factors related to demand, market and consumer which are underneath the building of any successful macro level branding strategies. Hence, the branding strategies which take into account the grass root factors related to demand, market and consumer are classified as Micro level branding strategies.

Spectrum of Branding Strategy

Contents

Types of Micro Branding Strategies

1. Branding Strategies Based on Geographical Reach

    1.1 Local Branding

    1.2 Regional Branding

    1.3 Global Branding

2. Branding Strategies Based on Target Income Group

    2.1 Super Rich Class Branding

    2.2 Rich Class Branding

    2.3 Middle Income Class Branding

    2.4 Poor Class Branding

3. Branding Strategies Based on Quality of Product

    3.1 Ultra Quality Branding

    3.2 Standard Quality Branding

    3.3 Common Quality Branding

4. Other Types of Micro Branding Strategies

   4.1 Value Branding Strategy
   4.2 Traditionalized Branding Strategy
   4.3 Trade Branding Strategy
   4.4 Gender Based Branding Strategy
   4.5 Age Based Branding Strategy
   4.6 Country (Province) Branding Strategy
   4.7 Ambassador Branding Strategy

Significance of Types of Micro Branding Strategies

Levels of Branding

   1. Product Level Branding
   2. Corporate Level Branding
   3. Technology Level Branding
   4. Green (Save the Planet) Branding

Hierarchy in Various Levels of Branding

Brand Architecture Possibilities

Types of Micro Branding Strategies

1. Branding Strategies Based on Geographical Reach

A Branding exercise may attempt to project a local, regional or global brand depending on the marketing strategy of the organization for that particular product or service.

1.1 Local Branding

Local Branding is pretty obvious in case of consumer products such as morning bread. In every small, mid or large size cities, there are several brands particular to the city. They provide freshness and intimacy to the consumer, which a regional or a global brand may not provide.

Many times, there are certain products which are consumed locally in a particular area only, say for example "Sarees" and "Canned and packed Sweets", which are mostly used in northern part of India respectively and diasporas of these populace elsewhere. Volume and size of the "Sarees" and "Canned and packed Sweets" market has attracted many players and as a result there are many brands locally present in the segment.

The connotation "local" has a wider meaning too, in the time of globalization. A product may be local to a country even. Marketing must define the scope and width of localness of a product before planning any branding exercise.

BPL brand is more a local brand to India, whereas Sanyo is a global brand acknowledged across continents. To enter in growing Indian market for consumer electronics and domestic appliances, Sanyo has planned to use BPL as partner in manufacturing as well as in marketing network. The strategy is to capture middle class by well known local brand BPL, while for attracting more sophisticated richer class, a global brand Sanyo is used. The significance of local and global brands is also material, in deciding and forging marketing alliance as part of broader marketing exercise.

Local branding is not about localization of global brands. It is about branding for a particular local area, which is the most likely market of the particular brand.

A Brand may be local to a city or few provinces or a country. If a brand is local to a city, entire marketing communications will limit to the confinement of the city while a brand is local to a country, all marketing communications will be spread across the country.

Characteristics of Local branding

- Proximity to consumer is a salient advantage

- Fresh supply

- Intimacy with consumer

- More coverage of local needs

1.2 Regional Branding

The scope of Regional Branding is wider than a local branding and narrower than global branding.

An organization having operations in entire India can think of promoting a regional brand, only for eastern part of the country. Another organization having operations in Asian continent can promote a regional brand for South East Asian countries.

Thus again, it is the marketing strategy of the organization, which will decide the regional scope of the particular branding exercise. But one constant fact is always involved in this process, that is the region selected must have some commonality or some common characteristics due to which it is more likely that the particular brand will sell more or will be easily accepted by the consumer of the particular region and will generate a good demand for the brand in the region.

Socio-cultural factors, ethnicity, linguistic similarity etc. are some of such common characteristics which are considered in selecting a Region.

Many often sales of an organization restricts to a particular region by coincidence or sales is outstandingly strong unintentionally in a particular region. In such situations the organization may think of expanding in some other region and this may necessitate a sort of regional branding for the region selected in the context.

For example Escort's tractor has a robust sales in the northern India compared to other regions. There might be uncountable number of business logics behind this fact, but what is obvious is that the company has a wider dealership network, more service centers and advertising campaign in the region. Definitely, it is a case of regional branding.

There is a similar case of Tata Motors and Ashok Leyland. Tata motor's sales is strong in northern India and Ashok Leyland 's sales is outstanding in southern India. This may not be totally attributed to the location of the manufacturing plants only as Tata's Plant is located in northern and also in western region whereas Leyland's Plant is located in southern region. But there are set of other reasons also, which may fall well within the phenomenon of regional branding.

Micro Branding Strategies

Characteristics of regional branding

- Capable to meet the need of particular Region or ethnicity

- Capable to convey marketing communication in people's own language

- Capable to meet those demands of customers, which a local or global brand can not meet

- Concentration of resources of the organization in the region

1.3 Global Branding

Global branding is very obvious in case of high technology products. Most of the global technology leaders have several globe tottering brands in their basket, may it be american information technology giants like Microsoft with Windows and Office, IBM with mainframes and DB2, Oracle with its Database software and Intel with its Pentium chips or German machine tool manufacturers or Japanese automotive giants like Toyota, Honda and Suzuki etc.

These brands are truly global brands. With advent and spread of Personal computers and internet, Microsoft's Windows and Internet Browser have penetrated into most of the villages worldwide. Similar is the case of Japanese automotive giant Honda. At one end, there is a Hero Honda motorcycle in most of the villages in India and at the other end, no American street can deny the presence of a Honda Bike.

Innovation and technology does not automatically spread across the globe but it is the planned approach of marketing, universal product design and creation & maintenance of reliable brands across continents, which make it possible.

All these global giants are not only best innovator, strategist and practitioner of technology, but are best in marketing and brand management too.

India or most of the developing nations may be having few or none truly global brands yet, meeting global quality. Ability to meet global customer demand and moreover creating reliable and durable global brands in true sense will decide the success of business houses of developing countries in globalization and WTO regime.

Characteristics of global Branding

- Latest technology

- High quality

- Marketing network across continents

- Scalable to regional and ethnic requirements

- High expenditure on marketing communications across continents

- High expenditure on research and localization

The exercise of branding at local, regional and global reach is in essence horizontal only. The strategy must be drawn vertically in each horizontal segments local, regional and global. Vertically possible segments in a geography are mountainous, hilly terrain, plains, islands, coastal areas and deserts etc. If the selected geography is divided into one or more vertical segments, branding strategy needs attention to all these segments. This is because of the fact that the need and reach of consumers from different vertical segment are different. Similarly, if the product is soil sensitive then possible vertical segments may be red soil, alluvial, black soil or sand etc. Some examples of soil sensitive products are seed and seedlings. The both are sensitive to type of soil.

2. Branding Strategies based on Target Income Group

Different cross-section of customers have a typically different need or demand as well as affordability and ways of ego satisfaction. The product which can satisfy the need of the poor, may satisfy the need of the rich too. But it may not provide ego satisfaction to the rich. Marketer must understand this typical consumer to consumer behavior and must design value added products as well as products which could satisfy attitudes also.

This is true in the case of branding too. A branding exercise has a typical cross section of consumer as target. Typically this cross section may be super rich class, rich class, middle income class or poor class.

For instance, Omega watches are targeted towards upper and rich class while HMT watches are targeted towards middle income class and poor class. Grasim and Raymond's textile division have segmented range of brands for premium class and middle income class.

2.1 Super Rich Class Branding

There are several global brands, which have sustained as favorite of the super rich class. Examples in Indian context could be Taj hotels, imported Mercedes cars etc.

Some of the common trait of these brands are like they have been first to offer the best technology or best hospitality and service. They have a long tradition of operations and loyal customers of successive generations.

These are the only brands in their respective segment, which could possibly provide the ego satisfaction to the super rich class combined with sense of security, privacy and intimacy. This all is not free of cost. Therefore these brands command a premium price, which is often exorbitantly higher than the nearest rivals. The materials used must be the costliest one, the design used must be the latest, most fancy and costliest and the most humble and reliable service must be provided to the super rich customers without bothering about the entire process of affordability. The Brand management of these legendary brands must be planned for a long term, since such successful brands are built only over a period of time.

Characteristics of super rich branding

- Costliest products among respective segment

- Legendary presence and loyalty across generations

- Prices are repulsive to non-rich

- Products must have best design, look and latest features

- Best quality products supported by best customer service

2.2 Rich Class Branding

High economic growth has injected a rich class in the society at a very fast pace in the recent years. This class is not only constantly searching for a change in models of their cars, motorbikes, home theatres, appliances and furniture etc., But it is the class, which is consuming offseason vegetables and fruits which are mostly imported, best clothes and shoes and is a regular visitor to newly opened fast food chains, shopping malls and multiplexes. They want to consume costly commodities at the earliest.

What is their tip to the marketer? Simply to quote "Your present Product is boring, cheap and out fashioned and have become common, though what we need is more exciting and interesting, costlier, more attractive and yet uncommon variety."

Access to this class is not difficult. They read English dailies, costly magazines including popular western magazines, travel often by air, often visits to international and other costly fast food chains, goes to resorts and star hotels for vacation.

All these behaviors help a marketer to find the best way to communicate with them easily.

Characteristics of rich class branding

- Latest lifestyle products

- Costly design

- Accommodative of constantly changing needs

- Influenced by cosmopolitan culture

- Targeted often by localized global brands

2.3 Middle Income Class Branding

Middle income class is a growing community in developing countries like India and China. Recently this class is the target class of multinational companies mainly in the segments like fast moving consumer goods, lifestyle and fashion segments and ready to eat foods and beverages segment etc.

This class can be further divided into urban and rural Middle class for marketing and branding purpose, because the behavior of urban and rural middle class are typically different many often.

Like any other class, the middle income class also has traits, which can be attributed to it.

Most captive catch word for this class is "affordable product". All products will have to qualify this criteria namely "affordable", to pass the acceptability by this class. The "affordability" will vary from product-to-product. In Indian context a Rs.2.2 lacs car is affordable, a home loan of Rs.5 lacs is an affordable home loan product, a Rs. 20k Personal computer is affordable, a Rs.1000/- Jeans Pant is affordable, a Rs.500/- branded shirt is affordable etc.

A marketer will have to understand this "affordability" factor in totality and in the context of the product. No wonder he will access a market of millions and millions of middle income class people, who love to buy these affordable products.

This class is also attracted by free after sales customer service, reliable and quality after sales service, exchange offers on old and used products, resale value and buy back options, packaged offers with discounts, payment in easy installment options or payment through credit cards, interest free loans at the door steps etc. A careful study of such options offered in the market shows that they are mostly targeted towards this middle class. There is intense competition among brands despite plethora of the schemes cited above as every brand seems to offer all the schemes available to the customer.

Characteristics of middle income class branding

- Affordable products in respective segment

- Easy financing and attractive schemes of finance

- Attractive schemes for customer retention like exchange offer

- High competition among many brands

- High volume of sales easily achieved

- Entry segment for multinational companies

1.4 Poor Class Branding

This class may be seen as lowest end of the market. This class is attracted by necessity combined with affordability of the product.

A product tagged with affordable price but least necessity or a necessary product with high price, both of these situations will repulse the demand.

An example of first case, which is a product of affordable price but of little necessity, is potato wafers in Indian rural markets. Howsoever cleverly low priced, wafers packets have not generated much demand in rural India.

Examples of second case, which is a product with necessity but priced high are, costly live saving medicines or devices and costly apartments. Many poor people die because they could not afford these high cost life saving medicines and there are people who live in substandard conditions because they can not afford highly priced apartments. Both the products, medicines and homes are necessity, but high price is acting as hurdle in sales realization.

There is a sizeable market of poor class and if a marketer ignores this class totally, a good market share may be lost.

Accessing this class through advertisements is not an easy task. This is because many of them do not read newspapers and magazines and many of them are illiterate also. Few effective ways to communicate them might be wall writings around Public places, hoardings at public facilities, Publicity through corner store shops and stalls in appropriate localities and distance rural places. Messages communicated with the help of popular film stars or other such popular personalities are best way to reach into this class. Finally, low pricing will also be a factor to realize a sizeable large volume of sales.

This class is often given a soft place in governance and is supported by public distribution system and other government initiative. The marketing to this class is definitely tantamount to competing with government sometimes.

Characteristics of poor class branding

- Low pricing with necessity

- Advertising should reach to poor class

- Literacy barrier must be crossed in communications

- Penetration in rural market is desired

- Publicity is preferred over other types of communications

- Competition with governmental agencies

- Wider distribution network required

3. Branding Strategy Based on Quality of the Product

Quality of the product (service) is deciding factor in fixing geographical reach as well as the target income group for the branding of the product (service). The above dependence is obvious. If the quality offered is world class definitely the geographical reach could be global and if the quality is poor then efforts of establishing a global type of brand will surely fail. Income wise, it is also seen that super rich and rich class people are highly quality conscious and accept only the products, which equal the best quality available in the market.

It is also to be acknowledged that branding is not done of high quality and costly items only, but branding is a necessity in case of commonly used products also, where either a standard quality is sufficient or quality is not an issue at all. The real factors in such cases are the size of the market and the key market players in the same segment.

There are cases, where the size of the market is in bulk and there are several players of big and small size active in the market. For example detergent washing powder, cold drinks, beverages, dish washing cakes, packed milk, hair shampoo, bath soaps, in all these cases there are many brands available in the market. Branding helps to capture more attention of the consumer and thereby resulting into bigger chunk of market share. The phenomena is quite evident from the fact that in detergent segment in Indian context, while the biggest FMCG majors like HLL, Proctor & Gamble, Nirma, Hipoline etc. are active with full efforts, there are so many other brands which are also present in the same segment like Ghadi, More, Plus etc. and moreover there are many unbranded local players too. They all exist in quality and cost matrix of the market.

Consumer electronics and home appliances segment also has fierce competition and has a large sales segment. Price range of the products are wide depending on features availability and brands. The phenomenon is true in case of cars two wheelers also. Here price range of the products are wider depending on features availability and brands compared to previous case.

Typically products can be classified based on quality they exhibit and branding of these products must be different in each case. The quality of a product could be ultra quality, standard quality or common quality. Branding based on quality of the products can thus be further classified into ultra quality branding, standard quality branding and common quality branding.

3.1 Ultra Quality Branding

The ultra quality branding is more prominent in case of high tech products, electronics consumer goods, capital goods, high tech project execution etc. Ultra quality is essential for bagging project where human security or high capital investment are involved or technical complexities are involved. Some of such areas are advanced medical equipment, real time software, space programs, defense production, aircrafts etc. Ultra quality is the most essential in developing market for these items.

Any corporation involved in such businesses must have ultra quality brands to flaunt.

Some of the ultra quality brands are Siemens in capital goods and medical equipment, Boeing and Air Bus in avionics , Falcon and Mirage in fighter aircrafts and Hitachi in engineering and marine production, Rolls Royce in engines. In ultra quality branding, previous success rates are deciding factors and it is not uncommon in marketing communications of such brands mention their success rate proudly.

These companies announce proudly their earlier success rate, which is invariable close to 100%. Ultra brand corporate in project like activities, or long term contractual work, has performance indices better than expected with least cost and time overrun.

Precision, security, reliability, advanced feature, trouble free continuous operations, robustness and hazard free operations are some of the top essential characteristics of these brands.

The cost factor is subservient and often is not a constraint in marketing such brands, as all the above mentioned qualities involve a considerable amount of investments and high cost.

Ultra quality branding is lasting investment. Most of the organizations, which own such brands capitalize over centuries and virtually monopolize their market. High impetus and investment in research and development is a common characteristic of these corporate. Generally these brands are not created in a short span of time, but it takes decades to make an ultra quality brand.

Spectrum of Branding Strategy

Characteristics of ultra quality branding

- High technology products are most suitable for this type of branding

- Costly research and design investments

- Reliable past performance is important

- Are built over time

- Less competition with few players

3.2 Standard Quality Branding

Standard qualities are set by either international standard organization like ISO and standardization organizations at nation level like ISI in India or by the industry itself. A set of norms are prescribed by governments also. For Real estate developers, there are requirements set by the government regarding parking space, open space and construction area but there are industry specific standards too, which may not be obligatory for example security, swimming pool, well equipped gymnasium, a shopping mall, polo ground to cite a few. In other cases like frost free refrigerators or flat and fully squared picture tube television sets etc. are mainly standards set by the industry.

Standard quality brands maintain at least such standards as followed by industry at the time, and they may acquire certain other qualities in addition.

If there are several players having ISO certification in the same segment, marketing and branding without the certification will be difficult. Besides equaling the competitors in standard qualities, one will have to have an edge over the others to create a brand. This edge is evident in cement brands as some players go for cement with red oxide with quality to fight rust or cement with quality to withstand local climatic conditions etc. Standard quality Brands will have stiff competition compared to ultra quality brands, as there will always be more players comparatively.

Characteristics of Standard quality branding

- Quality as per standard of the industry

- Additional quality has a role in competition

- Higher level of competition compared to ultra quality branding

3.3 Common Quality Branding

Besides major brands like Onida, LG, Samsung, BPL, Videocon, Toshiba and Sony in the color television sets, there are other well known brands like Weston, Texla, Beltek, Oscar, Crown and Igo etc., which share a sizeable part of television sets market. Quality is the main factor which divides these two sets of brands. Whereas, the first set of brands maintain standard qualities, the later set of brands depend on little obsolete technology and thereby a sharp fall in price.

They meet the demand of a different cross Section of the society or market, where a minimum quality is sufficient but the bonanza seen is the low price.

This is one good example of common quality branding. The common quality branding is efficient, when a little compromise with quality results into sharply declined Price range combined with the demand for cheaper brands. Hostels, middle class hotels and lodges, besides good number of families and working people are good market segment for low price branded color television sets. Fast moving consumer goods in personal care, beauty care, fast food, beverages are also the segments

Where besides high quality brands, common quality brands too compete in the market with good sales turnover. It is evident that in all these product segments chosen for common quality branding, the market is big, obsolescence is high and brand loyalty is low. Most important factor is price.

Characteristics of common quality branding

- Compromised approach between price and quality

- Highly competitive market with several players

- Suitable product segments are the one, with high obsolescence

4. Other Types of Micro Branding Strategies

4.1 Value Branding Strategy

Value branding is adopted by those organizations, which are engaged in social work or who are engaged in championing a social cause.

The essence of value branding is typically to exploit a social or a human value. In every society, there are certain social cause to work for, such as there are deprived people to be helped in many ways economically, educationally and sentimentally or there may be gender inequality or malnutrition among children.

There are many non profit private social organizations, non government organizations and also government bodies which champion such cause.

Brand "Red Cross" can be seen as pinnacle of value branding. "Cry" is another value brand in the area of helping estranged children. A part of proceed from the sales of branded pen, branded greeting cards and from sales of books of some publishers associated with "Cry" goes to the credit of "Cry". Here such pen manufacturer, greeting cards manufacturer and publications are trying value branding by exploiting the opportunity to help children.

Meeting the consumers needs beyond the business is also part of value branding. Free air supply at petrol pumps, welcome with a glass of drinking water at filling stations at distance locations on highways, catering service with warm smiles, child care, senior citizen's care and patients care in air travels are all part of value based branding, which always help in customer retention.

Characteristics of value branding

- Attention to social values

- Targets to enter into hearts through a human value

- Services beyond business

4.2 Traditionalized Branding Strategy

There are organizations in select few sectors like cosmetics, medicines and architecture, which emphasize on Ancient sciences and traditional knowledge base.

Some of the examples are Practice of 'Vastu Shastra', The ancient Indian architectural science or 'Feng Sui', the Chinese counterpart in architecture & construction or usage of age old herbal knowledge from various parts of the continents in the cosmetics production.

This phenomenon of branding products on ancient sciences to capture the attention of the market and people which have a strong faith in myths and age old sciences and practices depicted in ancient scriptures pertaining to various sphere of life may be classified as "Traditionalized Branding".

Fast moving herbal cosmetics in the personal care segment are fast replacing chemically manufactured cosmetics products. Herbal products manufacturers, while branding their products highlight, the nature friendly characteristics of the herbs and characteristics of the herbs, which do not have any side effects.

There are many builders, who promote themselves as builder of houses and townships built according to ancient old architectural science "The Vastu Shastra". Vastu shastra advocates prosperity, piece of mind and fortune of a person also depends upon the construction. These principles have been part of civilizations and are again being accepted with great respect by a section of society.

Similarly in para-medical sciences also, traditional way of cure is being exploited by many like Kerala's ayurvedic massage therapy, acupressure and many other therapies.

Characteristics of traditionalized branding

- Importance to ancient sciences

- Nature friendly advocacy

- Believe in super natural forces

4.3 Trade Branding Strategy

Branding is often construed as synonym of consumer branding, which presumes that the brand is consumed by a wide cross section of the society. But it is not true always. There are certain products mostly industrial products which are not consumed by the society directly, but are consumed by a particular industry. Automobile ancillaries like forgings, castings etc. or parts of capital goods or railways components are some of the products, which are consumed directly by respective industry and not by society.

Hence the branding of such products must be exercised keeping in mind this fact and target must be the concerned industry rather than public.

Typically this type of branding communication use specific magazines and journals concerned to the sector and visit respective trade fairs. Besides this, visits by company personnel to the consuming industries, distribution of company published brochures to prospective consumers and training workshops for the technicians also, are the ways to promote industry specific products. This type of branding comes under the ambit of trade branding.

The aim of trade branding is to reach every link in the concerned trade from manufacturers, to distributors, to shops and to technical personnel. Branding in pharmaceuticals sector is also a good example of trade branding. Branding strategy for pharmaceuticals is typically different in terms of market segmentation. The typical segments may be cardiology, nephrology, therapeutics or oncology etc. The complication of segmentation is typically different in any specialized industrial sector also, may it be computing, robotics, space technology or thermal. Thus in trade branding strategy, understanding and creating segment is essential to succeed.

Another type of branding under the ambit of trade branding is branding of export oriented products and units. There are certain products, which are consumed abroad and there are certain manufacturing facilities, which are dedicated to export demands. Such products and units must be branded in the export market.

Bicycle Indian manufacturers have created a strong brand in African and European countries, which is a good example of export branding. Today Indian software service providers Like TCS, Infosys and Wipro are at par with other international software service brands like IBM, Accenture and EDS. This is also an example of strong export trade branding.

Micro Branding Strategies

Characteristics of trade branding

- Specific to a trade or a market

- Industry to industry communications

- Industry to distributors communication

- Not consumed by people directly

4.4 Gender Based Branding Strategy

A Product may be consumed by either gender (by men or by women) or it can be consumed by a particular gender (either by men or either by women alone). Thus, there are two types of the products based on the gender based consumption pattern, omni and gender specific.

Gender based branding is necessity in case of second type of products, which are designed to be consumed by a particular gender only. There are masculine products like shaving kits and aftershave lotion, men's range of garments, cosmetics. Then, there are feminine products like jewelries, women's range of garments, cosmetics, magazines and beauty products.

Thus, the products must be conceived, designed, marketed and branded keeping in mind the targeted gender also. One important dimension of gender specific products is the choice. Even though a product may be designed for a particular gender, But the choice may be of the opposite gender. Few specific examples are after shave lotion or perfume spray. After must be liked by women. Similarly in case of perfumes, even shave lotion is targeted for men but it is likely that the smell though targeted for women, but the choice of men can not be ignored. Thus the choice dimension must not be ignored while designing a gender based product.

There are choice less gender specific products like women's beauty care or women's gymnasium equipment. These products must be designed to suit skin and physique of the women respectively and do not give any choice to opposite gender.

Choice dimension is not only important in design of gender specific products, But it is also important in selecting proper media for communication and also in choosing a suitable brand name, slogan or ambassador. The gender with dominant choice must be preferred. Model Cindy Crawford, one among select few costly ambassadors in the world, in the campaign for Omega watches with male wrist watch on her wrist is an example of gender with dominant choice.

Once the target gender is defined, branding goals should also be defined in terms of geographical reach i.e. whether to promote a local, a regional or a global brand and in terms of targeted income group i.e. whether to promote a brand for rich class, middle income group or poor class.

Gender based branding is also relevant in case of products, which are consumed by either gender but marketing organization targets a specific gender. The organization may opt either to fortify the Brand in the same gender, where it is strongly present or it may opt to strengthen its position in the gender where it has a weaker presence or it may opt for strengthening its position in both. Once this goal is set, The branding must proceed accordingly. There are gender preferred jargon, gender preferred ambassadors, gender preferred locations and joints, all these must be studied well to make an entry into consumers of specific gender.

Characteristics of gender based branding

- Targets a particular gender

- Analysis of gender wise consumption of the products required

- Gender with dominant choice is more important in decisions made design, manufacture and sales

4.5 Age Based Branding Strategy

There are two types of products in the context of age groups. The first type of the products is, those Products which are consumed equally (or proportionately) and uniformly across the various age groups of a society. The second type is, of those products which are more likely to be consumed by a particular age group.

The age based branding is necessity in the branding of second type of the products. The age group which is more likely to consume the product, must be targeted through appropriate means and branding exercise must be carried keeping the relevant age group in the center.

Magazines are one example of age sensitive products. On the newsstand, one finds magazines for children, magazines for young and magazines for senior citizen. Housing loans and pension funds are few financial products, which are more likely to be availed by middle age group. Such products must be structured, marketed and branded after understanding the need and financial capacity of the middle age group of the targeted society.

One age group is actually not independent, which is the children group. Any branding for this group, must keep in mind that this group' decisions are molded and are dependent on their parents decision. Various age group have their own craze, energy levels, hobbies and ideals. The characteristics of the targeted age group must be understood, well before branding a product for that specific age group.

Age based branding is also relevant in case of products, which are consumed by various age groups together but the a marketer decides to target a particular age group on some hypothesis of his own thinking. Suppose, according to the marketer the consumption capacity of a typical age group is much more than the present consumption by the group. Thus he finds a market opportunity there. It is natural that he will go for a brand targeted to that specific age group identified by him.

In such cases, consumption pattern must be quantified among various age groups to know, which age group consumes the brand in what proportion or percentage. The data will guide to set the goals for marketing and for branding. Branding here must be done in two factors in the mind. Firstly, branding must retain the age group which consumes most and secondly, branding must aim to improve the customer base in the age group which do not consume the brand in expected proportion, despite the capacity.

Characteristics of age based branding

- Targets a particular age group

- Analysis of age group wise consumption pattern is required

Age can also be segmented into ancient age, medieval age, modern age and future age. This segmentation is seen in case of entertainment products like comics, movies and TV serials.

4.6 Country (Province) Branding Strategy

Country branding is much evident in developing Asian countries like Taiwan, Korea, Mauritius, Singapore or lately in China and India, in the way they have been projected by native governments and various agencies for attracting foreign direct investments and as outsourcing hub for cheaper but quality manufacturing or service rendering. As a consequence of this exercise these countries have been favored globally in respective areas and have attracted huge foreign direct investments or have emerged as preferred outsourcing hub. Emergence of China as manufacturing outsourcing country and India as outsourcing hub of IT and software related services are some of the most recent and prominent examples of country branding.

Such successes have been achieved by promulgating encouraging governmental policies like creation of special economic zones (S.E.Z.) and providing infra-structural support, tax incentives etc. to the units which are established in such zones in case of China and creation of software export zones and similar benefits as mentioned above to the software service providers working from such zones in case of India. Incentives are also available to the export oriented units located otherwise also.

Actually the role of government is far beyond such industrial policies. Creating a world class work force by opening up technical education to private players and by opening more institutes of repute in government control or increasing the seats in existing important institutes are all another country level plannings.

Most important is creating a global awareness of these policies and resources so that the message is herd in the world community. Government efforts and negotiations at diplomatic levels, interactions and efforts by domestic chambers of commerce through meets and trade fairs etc. are part of the country branding exercise.

These countries are also helped by opinion of credit rating agencies like CRISIL and Standard & Poor, international monitory agencies like World Bank, International Monetary Fund, Asian Development Bank and other giant banking and investing incorporations. Government role is again important here as the opinions of such agencies are dependent on the sovereign's political stability, economic and industrial policies and natural resources and it's management. Declaration of policies in harmony with interest of such international monitory bodies helps a nation to become a preferred destination for economic activities.

Tourism is one Industry, which can be called as catalyst for country branding. Few decades ago, Mauritius (An island country in Indian ocean) used country level branding of itself to project it as heaven of travelers and tourists. The result had two components direct and indirect. As a direct Result the island became one of the most favorite place for tourists. Considerable amount of currency is earned from tourism to stem the economy. But there was indirect impact also. The country also became heaven for the investment arms of the international banks and other financial institutions, helped with little additional efforts like tax concessions.

Moreover, Sri Lanka, Cambodia, Maldives and India are also in process of country branding to attract more tourists and to earn more foreign currency consequently. The part of this branding exercise are to protect important monuments and heritages, create tourism infrastructure, cultural interactions through government sponsored and privately sponsored activities and advertisements, which are again government sponsored and privately sponsored.

In government sector, there are cultural councils responsible for cultural interaction, student exchange with the rest of the world, there is tourism ministry and tourism development board and there are public enterprises in hospitality sector. All the above mentioned bodies, conduct national and international events and repeatedly insert advertisements which promote tourism in the country.

Hosting of international prestigious sports events like asian games or Olympics and other international tournaments are also part of country branding. These type of events bring in people across cultures together and let them know each other in a better way, which forges a relationship.

Characteristics of country branding

- Government sponsorship

- Infrastructure development for candidate industry

- Resources available in abundance and throughout the country

Province Branding

Often the same process as in case of country branding, is worked out at province level instead of at the Sovereign level, which could be called "Province Branding ".

For example, states like Orissa and Jharkhand in India are fast on the way of attracting foreign direct investment through branding their province as naturally most resourceful zones in terms of mines and mineral resources, investor friendly industrial policies and infrastructure development. It will not be a surprise, if these province attract huge FDI in near future and tread a path of rapid industrial growth, because both domestic and international mining and metal manufacturing giants have evinced interest in establishing plants.

Tourism is major source of revenue of the Indian provinces of Kerala and Goa, which are good example of province branding in tourism Sector. These provinces have been ahead of the rest of the country in branding themselves as tourists favorite destination or rather paradise. As a result these provinces attract largest number of tourists. All this has been possible because of the natural beauty of such places, and also because of the development of tourism infrastructure, government's role in promoting peoples participation such as encouraging people to accommodate few tourists in their house during peak season or otherwise etc.

Characteristics of province branding

- Provincial government sponsorship

- Infrastructure development for candidate industry throughout province

- Resources available in abundance and throughout the province

Country branding and province branding has a key role to play in economic growth of the developing and under developed countries. Every such country and province must select one or more key industries to be promoted at the country or province level.

The candidate industry for country level branding must be selected carefully. Few factors which will help here are such as natural resources available in abundance and in most of the parts of the country, employment prospects, cost of infrastructure development and economic benefits thereof, human resources, skills of human resources and cost of further skill development and training of the human resources etc.

Today India is most leading country in rendering information Technology enabled services or China is foremost Country in manufacturing outsourcing. Even other countries can think to join them and compete with them with creating a similar infrastructure and trained human force.

Developing nations, which have a better educational infrastructure, a pool of technically qualified manpower and natural resources needed for industrial production, but which have not capitalized on these resources available, must start country branding by taking such initiatives as selecting candidate industry for country level branding, developing industrial infrastructure, initiatives to attract FDI and initiatives to increase public participation in industrial development etc. to tread a path of rapid industrial growth.

For the nations, which do not have pool of technically qualified manpower or natural resources for industrialization, there are economic activities which do not require technically qualified human resources, rather they need crafting skills like diamond cutting and polishing, pottery, apparel knitting, wood working, brass, bronze and other metal wares, agriculture, aquaculture, tourism, sports, transport and many more skills and industries. These crafts and industries are presently localized to particular places but, with governmental support, these crafts and industries can also be intensified and spread to other regions or provinces or countries as well, resulting into employment and economic growth in respective regions.

Such nations must select few candidate crafts or industries for country branding and take such initiatives as developing skills among people through training, providing financial support and raw materials and marketing support to become global hub for selected industry.

4.7 Ambassador Branding Strategy

Super stars like Maradona, Tendulkar and Pierce Brosnan are super Brands too. Individual's popularity is saleable commodity today. The worth of individual's popularity is reflected into individual's brand Value.

Super Stars Maradona, Tendulkar and Pierce Brosnan are best paid brand ambassadors in contemporary world. Business brands like to associate cachet of these super brand ambassadors desperately and therefore they are paid a very high contract money. The association of such super brand ambassadors with any business brand, immediately shoots the brand up in the ladder and makes it a high profile brand in shortest possible time.

Besides global individual brands, every ethnicity has its own idols. Thus there is choice for choosing an effective Brand ambassador. The brand ambassador must be chosen carefully to suit the target segment of the market for a brand. The geographical reach of the brand and target income group must be defined well before selecting a brand ambassador.

The individual brands must also be aware of their strength suitability to a particular business brand before entering into any contract of brand promotion. This is because the success of the promotion will have impact on the future value and status of these individual brands.

Characteristics of ambassador branding

- Aims to fortify a brand by popularity of a star personality

- Best means to promote a brand in shortest possible time

Significance of Types of Micro Branding Strategies

The understanding of these classifications of branding strategies will help an organization in many ways in creating an effective brand and manage efficiently the existing brands.

A deep understanding of various types of branding will help an organization in following activities,

1. Positioning a new brand

2. To acquire other new types of brands which the organization may not be having currently in its brand portfolio and thus to extend its brand line inorganically.

3. To bring new products under a brand.

4. To select proper media for brand promotion.

5. To select most suitable brand symbol, slogan or ambassador etc.

6. Premium of the brand i.e. the premium pricing of the products under the brand.

7. Modifying products design under a brand.

8. Deciding technology acquisition for new range of products under a brand.

9. Helping organizations to profit from and to promote the ancient and traditional knowledge of humanity such as ancient herbal or architectural sciences.

10. Helping political masters of a country (province) to promote their territory as leader in particular business activity and generate economic resources.

11. Helping NGO's and other social entities to project them as a value based organization.

Levels of Branding and Brand Architecture

Levels of branding define the brand architecture. A well known brand architecture is product brands under umbrella of a corporate brand. The relationship and affinity between the product brand and the corporate brand is deciding factor in resource sharing and allocation between corporate branding and product branding. However there are other brand architecture, which are possible with paradigm shift in branding with increased complexity in structure of market, demand, consumer, technology, marketing and branding.

An effort has been done to understand various other possible levels at which branding can be done in an environment of complex relationship between consumer, product, technology, corporate and social issues.

Branding efforts are oriented towards the object of the brand. Commonly the object of a brand is a product or a commodity. For example, the object of the brand Van Hussein is shirt or the object of the brand Bata is shoe or footwear. Both, the shirt and the shoe are a product or a commodity.

Often we see advertisements, which mention the name of the corporate more prominently than any product or on occasions the marketing communications mention just the corporate name. This is clearly case of branding the corporate. The object of the corporate branding is corporate itself. The main ambition of the corporate branding is to distinguish itself from other existing business rivals or to obviate any possible newcomer and position itself as well established.

This phenomenon of corporate branding compels one to contemplate about other various levels, at which branding could be possible.

The phenomenon of advancement in technology, increasing competition in domestic and global horizons, increasing business complexities in rapidly growing economic parameters, overexploitation of nature, deteriorating environmental conditions have changed every business perspective including branding strategies also. The brand building has also adapted to these factors and no more the object of the branding is restricted to products and corporate only.

Possibilities of levels at which, branding strategy can be built is listed below and discussed in following paragraphs.

Spectrum of Branding Strategy

1. Product Level Branding

2. Corporate Level Branding

3. Technology Level Branding

4. Green (Save-The-Planet) Branding

Basically the branding efforts at one level have some cascading effect on other levels. For example, branding efforts at the corporate level branding has a cascading impact on product level branding, which is obvious from the fact that, a product level brand is automatically promoted, in tandem with any corporate level branding.

If, a strong image of an enterprise is established in the public eye by an effective corporate branding, the public accepts the product brands of such enterprise in great respect with little or no efforts. Thus there is a hierarchical relationship in the various levels of the branding as listed above. The efforts of the branding at a higher level have a positive impact on the lower level of the branding too.

1. Product Level Branding

The object of product level branding is a product or closely related multiple products. Colgate is a good example of a product level brand, the object of which is toothpaste.

The new stylish entrants in ready-to-wear apparel segment like Globus, Pantaloon, Color Plus, and Wearhouse etc. are examples of retail chain brands which sell closely related many product brands, the object which is men's and women's wear. Similar is the case of herbal cosmetics player like Ayur or cosmetics players like Emami or Lakme, which offer a number of closely related products under one Brand. The closely related products can be identified as one product class. Product level branding is probably the lowest possible level of branding.

Product brands must be understood well in terms of its geographical reach, target income group in making the brand successful.

In fast food segment, there are Players like McDonalds and Pepsi, the geographical reach of which is global and Haldiram, which is a regional Player.

Spectrum of Branding Strategy

Coca Cola is one of the most well known global brand, which is almost significantly present in only one product class, that is soft drinks.

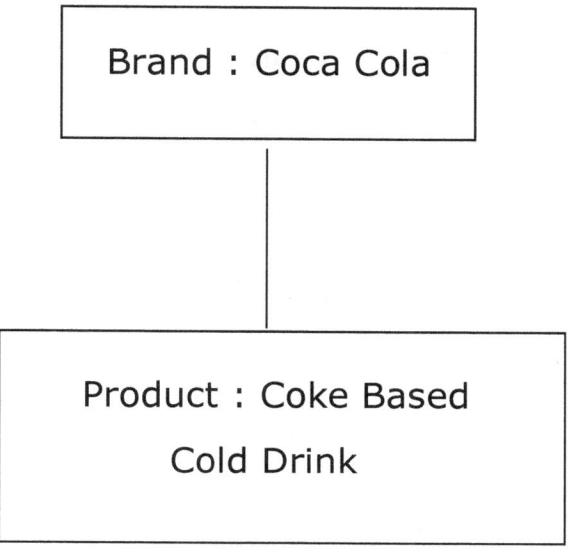

Maruti brand, which is brand that owns most sold cars in India, is also a single product brand which deals only in cars.

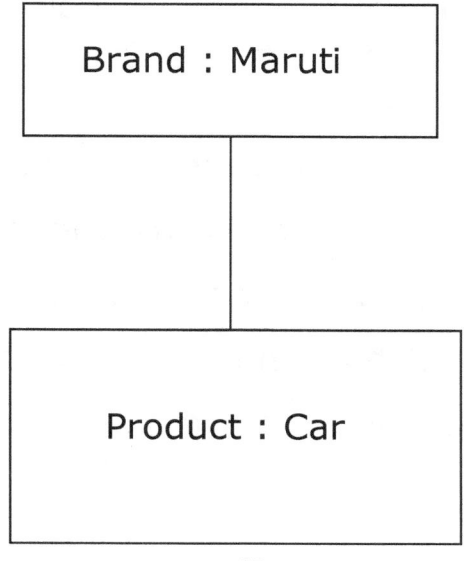

Single product branding is effective when the size of the Market is huge and there are few competitors in the market.

Lakme and Ayur are brands with multiple products in their fold. These brands are example of multi product brands.

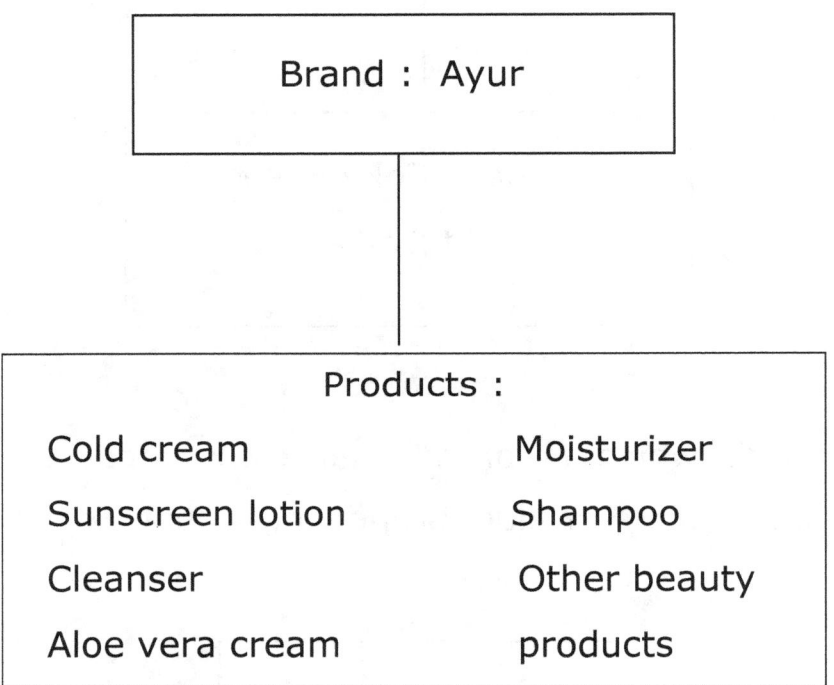

Some of the Best and most admired brands are single product brands. Single product brand allows the organization to be focused, but there is always a threat of losing a share when a new entrant makes a debut. The natural outcome of this threat is, opening up for closely related multiple products branding.

2. Corporate Level Branding

Corporate branding is natural for large corporate with diversified interest and a long time presence. A marketing communication, most visible component of which is, the corporate itself, is part of corporate level branding. It is beginning of the process by which a lasting impression of the organization is tried to be loaded into the memory of the people. The process is helped by a popular short name for the organization and a popular slogan or symbol.

Example of some of the ubiquitous corporate names are Tata, JK, Essar, Reliance in Indian context and Ford, Sony, IBM etc. in global context.

Example of some of the popular corporate slogans are "Intel Inside" of Intel Corporation of U.S.A., "Trusted Medicines, Touching Lives" of Ranbaxy, "The Positive Attitude" of Essar, "Affordable Computer Education, Worldwide" of SSI Ltd. etc. of India.

Once these lasting corporate names, slogans, symbols are heavily loaded into the memory of public, these are repeated in every marketing communication from the organization, in exactly same form, so as to remind the market that we are present in this segment also. An outstanding example of this is, advertisements of Intel Corporation, U.S.A., the biggest chipmaker of the world, which invariably mention the slogan "Intel Inside" in its corporate communications.

The pride of a corporate brand is quite obvious in campaigns of the group companies of the Tata group, India. Irrespective of the products, which may be automobiles, chemicals, tea or salt, there is a space depicting in bold letters "A TATA Product". This is the message to the public that the quality you trust somewhere in our other products is present here also.

The major advantage of corporate branding is easy diversification or new product launch under the same brand. By virtue of prolonged and persistent advocacy of success and excellence of an organization in media and its successful presence in many market segments, the corporate entity becomes a symbol of trust and blind reliability among the people.

There are certain sectors where the branding practice is only at the corporate level. Indian PSU Banks are one such example.

Allahabad bank, Corporation bank or Vijaya bank, they all depend on their glorious existence of several decades. These banking entities boast on efficient and complaint free service to the public rather than their banking products, which are more or less similar in each case. Other candidate sectors for corporate branding are school education with brand Like DPS (Delhi Public School), coaching institutes with brands like Aakash Institute, FIIT-JEE, Professional tutorials etc. and private sector universities with brand like Amity university.

The reason for corporate branding in such sectors is very clear. The products they offer are hardly any different from competitors. They also provide same banking products or entrance coaching or a degree, which other players are also offering in exactly same form.

The difference lies in the name only and which is the reason for the corporate branding. Corporate brands are built in two ways, first is practiced by large and diversified business houses or conglomerates like Tata in India. These corporate are pioneers and were first few responsible for industrialization of the economy. Naturally they have popularity, which is often carried through generation by generation. Such organizations become iconic corporate brands with efforts like corporate social responsibilities, charity work and value based sponsorship combined with advertisement in media.

There is second way also, which is evolutionary way of corporate branding. Evolutionary way of corporate branding is practiced by a relatively small organization working in one or very few areas with strong presence along with a popular brand, but are ambitious to grow large.

Glaring example of an evolutionary corporate branding is "Reliance group". Starting with a petrochemical business within few decades, the Reliance group has become largest business group of India leaving behind several business houses which have history of several generations in Indian business. Today Reliance is present in refineries, textile, retail, power, finance, infrastructure and telecommunication. Another but a slow growing evolutionary corporate brand in India is "Godrej" brand. Starting just with a strong lock brand, the Godrej group has grown to a large size diversified group having strong presence and popular brands in office and home furniture, refrigerators & other home appliances, soaps, hair dye, real estate, beverages, wheat flour and other FMCG products. Today, Godrej commands a considerable respect in these business areas in the country.

Spectrum of Branding Strategy

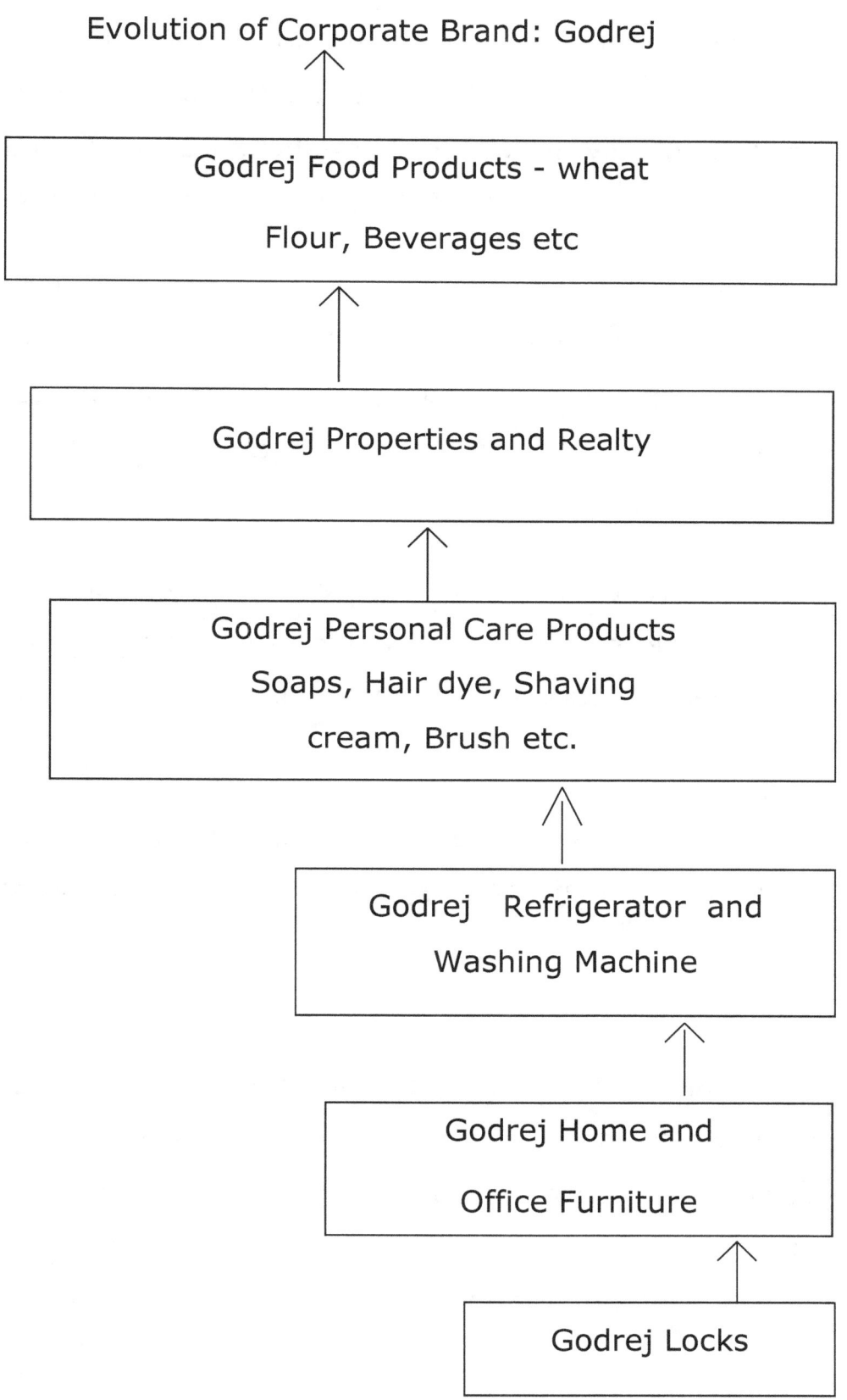

The evolutionary way to a corporate brand is done in steps. First a product brand is made success, in this example Godrej locks. Secondly, new related products are launched under same brand name, in this example Godrej office and home furniture.

Next step is to diversify in totally new area of business activity, In this example diversification of Godrej in refrigerators, personal care products and beverages.

Lastly, a good campaign and proportionate real physical efforts to fulfill the promises mentioned in the campaigns is initiated, which lead to success of many business under one name.

Finally a corporate brand is established, in the present example, Godrej is today an admirable corporate brand in India.

The main advantage of corporate branding is thus the ease with which diversification in other business areas can be achieved. The other advantage of corporate Brand is easy arrangement of finance either domestic or foreign, enhanced shareholder value, and a higher premium on equity capital on stock exchanges allowing group companies to capitalize on equity holdings.

Essar group is likely to be an example among Indian business houses, which is in making of a giant corporate brand in line with Tata or Ambanies. Besides its flagship companies Essar steel and Essar Shipping, its presence in high growth areas and further expansion plans through acquisitions and diversifications are ambitious. Essar construction in engineering and construction, Essar oil in refineries and fuel oil distribution, Essar power in electricity production and distribution and Essar telecom in telecommunication and mobile service are group companies of the Essar group. With presence in all these high growth areas in Indian context, Essar group is set to rise as a giant engineering group and moreover a very much known corporate in India.

Characteristics of corporate branding

- Portrays a corporate name as symbol of quality and trust

- Is built over a period of time

Micro Branding Strategies

- Co-exists with multiple product brands

- Corporate Brand's name or symbol appears in the product brands communications

- Wider geographical reach

- Products across different segments get benefit of the corporate branding

3. Technology Level Branding

It is the Japanese corporate armed with superior technology brands, who have conquered the global markets & western counterparts. It is corporate 's contribution that Japan is one of the richest country in the world today, notwithstanding, its peril during world war. From hi-tech electronics goods to high performance automobile products to easy to use consumer goods, a series of inventions and breakthrough technology achievement have given wings to Japanese products to spread across globe at affordable cost and widespread acceptability due to high quality.

Technology branding occurs when a new critical technology replaces an existing technology with broadly perceivable enhancements in the next generation products compared to present age products, that too not at a very high cost.

In many cases, for example mobile handsets or computing devices, enhanced models have been made available at a lower price compared to the present devices. In western and other rich countries, plasma television sets are replacing the present sets. Plasma television sets are rather costly to Indian markets and penetration is very low.

If a breakthrough technology is achieved and low cost Plasma television sets roll into the markets, It will not be surprising that western manufacturers sell off their present television sets component manufacturing plants to their eastern counterparts and penetration of plasma television sets in Indian market drastically increases. Only time is to tell, if it is going to be a Japanese corporation again to achieve this breakthrough technology.

The object of the technology branding is not a product or a corporate, But its a breakthrough technology or a new technology. A breakthrough technology or new technology improves performance drastically.

Hybrid seeds, radial tire, twin blades, digital devices like DVD, high strength alloys, unix based operating systems, all are few examples of breakthrough technology, which have easily penetrated the markets once price barrier has been achieved. Color xerox, mobile telephony, internet and relational database management systems are recent few examples of new technologies, which have paved a new range of business opportunities. Difference between breakthrough technology and new technology is simple. If cost of a new technology is reduced to a such a level that it's products can be made available at a much lower price in market over a wide geography, then it can be said that breakthrough technology has been achieved.

Non availability of enough crude oil within its territories, has a deep impact on India's foreign exchange and growth. There are vehicles designed to run on ethanol alone in addition to petrol run vehicles in Brazil, a sugar rich country. Even India can think on the same line, being one of the largest producer of cane sugar. The cost competitiveness of ethanol versus petrol will govern the issue. It is time for the governments and automobile manufacturers to give a serious thought on new technology vehicles running on ethanol alone. If sugar manufacturers, automobile manufacturers, oil marketing companies and government agencies lobby for promotion of ethanol alone automobiles in India, it will be a fit example of beginning of technology branding.

Bio technology is one area where technology branding appears to be seen in the industry. The market is flushed with genetically modified seeds and biotech medicines. Governments, people, farmers, medical practitioners and consumers have been made aware of advantages of these hi technology seeds and medicines. As a result these products command a good demand today. The manufacturing companies in this sector seem to promote the common interest that is bio-technology. The process of technology branding of bio technology is explained with flow diagram as under

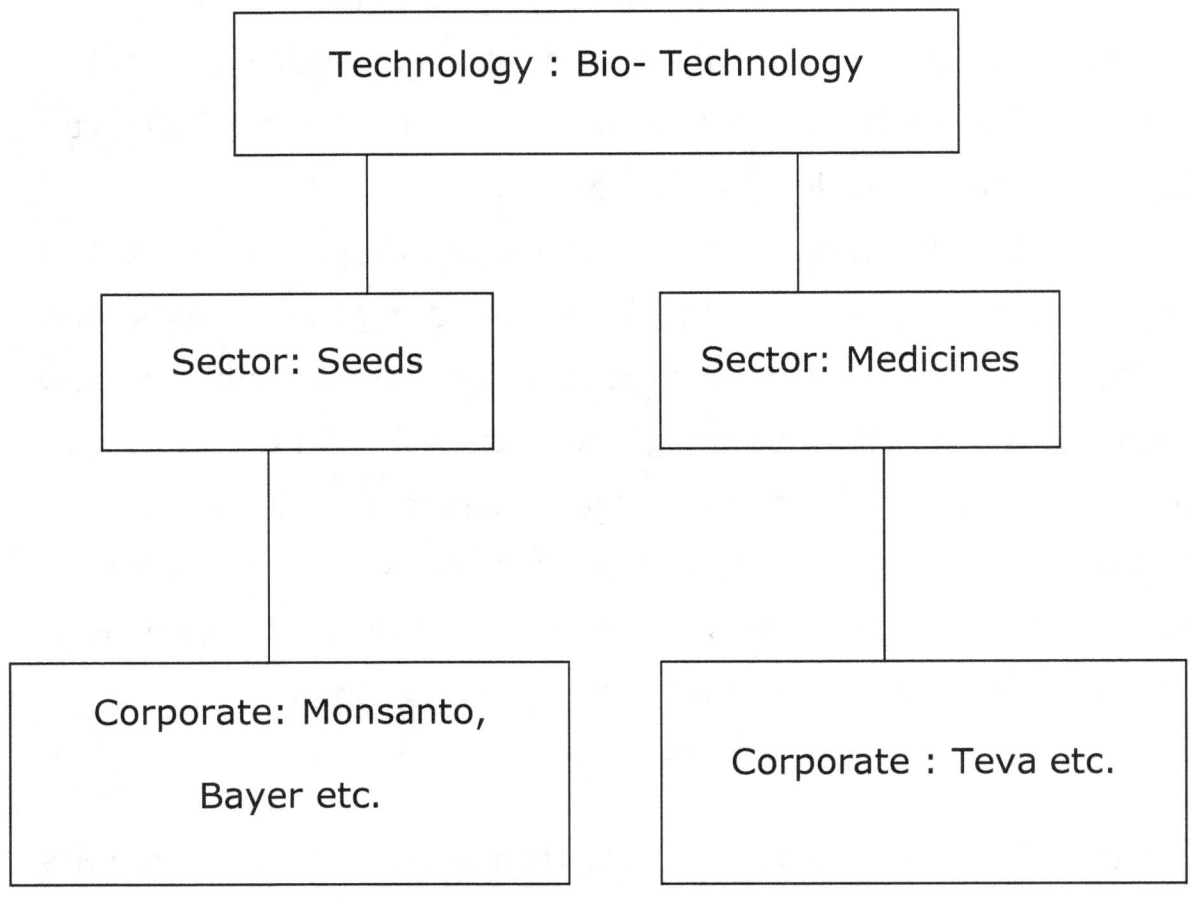

Digital technology is another technology area where technology branding appears to be seen in the industry. These companies actively promote the common interest that is digital technology. Digital technology has penetrated not only in business organizations but in governance also. This penetration

is made possible in short span of time not only by market demand but also by influencing the business organizations and Politicians.

Presence of digital technology in every sphere of life is evident in the flow chart shown below.

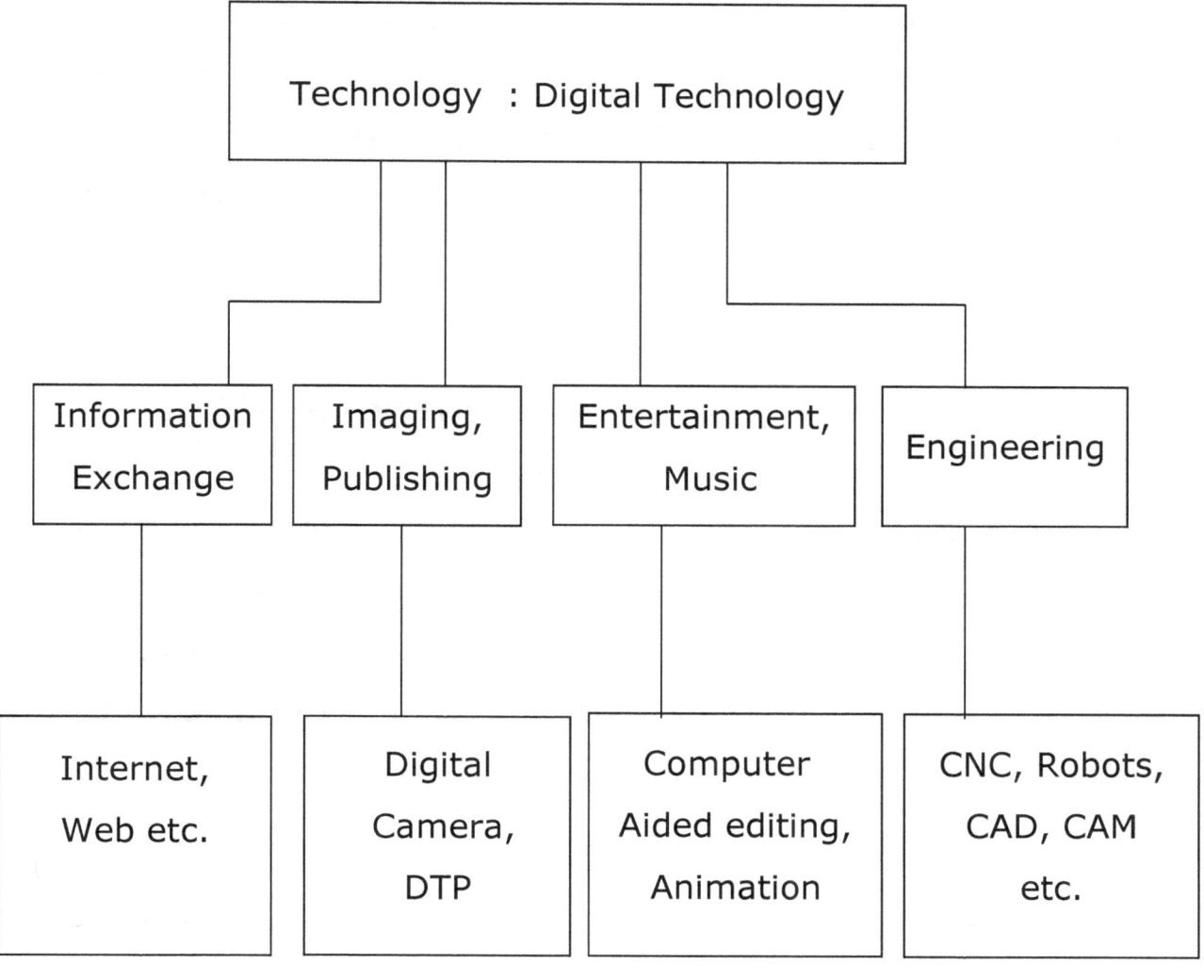

4. Green Level Branding

The Branding, which is based on such appeal as save environment, reduce pollution level, shun deforestation, preserve soil, preserve natural habitat etc. is green branding. Save environment, shun deforestation, preserve soil, preserve natural habitat are few slogans, which propel green branding.

Green branding is quite similar to technology branding, but is much wider than branding a single technology. Another obvious difference is, that a green brand is acceptable to society at a high premium on the cost, which may not be acceptable in case of all technology brands.

The improved performance and a perceivable benevolent effect caused by a technology is the real issue in the technology, But in case of green branding, the real issue is whether it protects environment or planet as a whole. There is a social cause behind green branding. Therefore green causes get vehement support from governmental and other agencies, which allow green brands to spread, even at a high cost.

Few examples of green brands are costly apartments and housing schemes and townships coming amidst forest like environment being artificially created by plantation, located mainly close to heavily populated metro cities. Such schemes depend on factors such as clean and pure air to breathe, least noise pollution, clean water to drink and forested surrounding, which all are green causes. These apartments are also good example of the kind of high premium commanded by green branding. The apartments in Forest city of Kukreja Builders in proximity of New Delhi, are priced starting with Rs. 10 Millions, which is exorbitant in Indian context. It is the lush green landscaping, planted forests, pollution free and noise free environment, which is attracting the rich, which they do not find in concrete jungles of the metropolitan cities. Standards and norms of ISO are not the limit, it is the extra bit of luxurious greenery, which will attract the buyer.

The industry has a much vast green cause list such as protect ozone layer, reduce dependence on non renewable natural resources e.g. crude oil, coal etc., preserve ecosystem and biodiversity, replace devices which cause harmful radiations and much more. A lot of efforts have been done to develop new green technologies. Products and technologies based on solar energy or wind energy have been conceived. CFC free refrigerators help in protecting ozone layer. Hydro power plants reduce dependence on thermal power plants running on coal.

Biodegradable materials are replacing non degradable materials like plastics.

Green branding is not about promoting and exploiting potential of a single technology, But is about a green cause. One of the finest example would be carbon emission reduction agreement among developed and underdeveloped nations. Industrial organization are required to reduce carbon emission in a defined quantity measured in units called Carbon Emission reduction points (CER points). If the organizations of developed nations could not reduce carbon emission in required units, they can purchase it from the organizations of underdeveloped nations against prices agreed. The intension of this policy is clear, which is to promote the practice of accumulating CER points resulting into less polluted atmosphere for which industry will be getting monitory benefit also.

Power plants, refineries, steel plants, automotive textile and numerous other types of enterprises of underdeveloped nations like India, are ready to exploit the benefits of trading in CER Points and many are implementing technologies that have effect of reducing carbon emission. In power sector, power Plants and power transmission companies can accumulate CER points by energy efficiency and by use of renewable energy resources, sugar complexes by use of captive plants run on renewable fuel, mining sector like aluminum ore mines by gas capture and steel mines and refineries by fuel switching and energy efficiency respectively.

Green cause and branding does not enhance the quality of the product directly. Rather the organization, which involve themselves in the green cause get benefited in two ways. Firstly, they will encash on the CER points accumulated for a handsome money and secondly, the corporate image and corporate brand value will enhance. Many often, they will become select suppliers of the green cause champions and governments.

Green level of branding will encourage those technologies which are responsible for a green cause such as reduction in carbon emission in the discussions above. There are several issues pertaining to protection of our planet and survival. Green branding takes up an issue and will support many technologies involved in the cause. These all technologies improve the overall environment such that production process achieve a minimum level of interference in our environmental system and maximum level of preservation of the environment. The involved technologies will be implemented in various organization. The flow process is explained here by a diagram.

Micro Branding Strategies

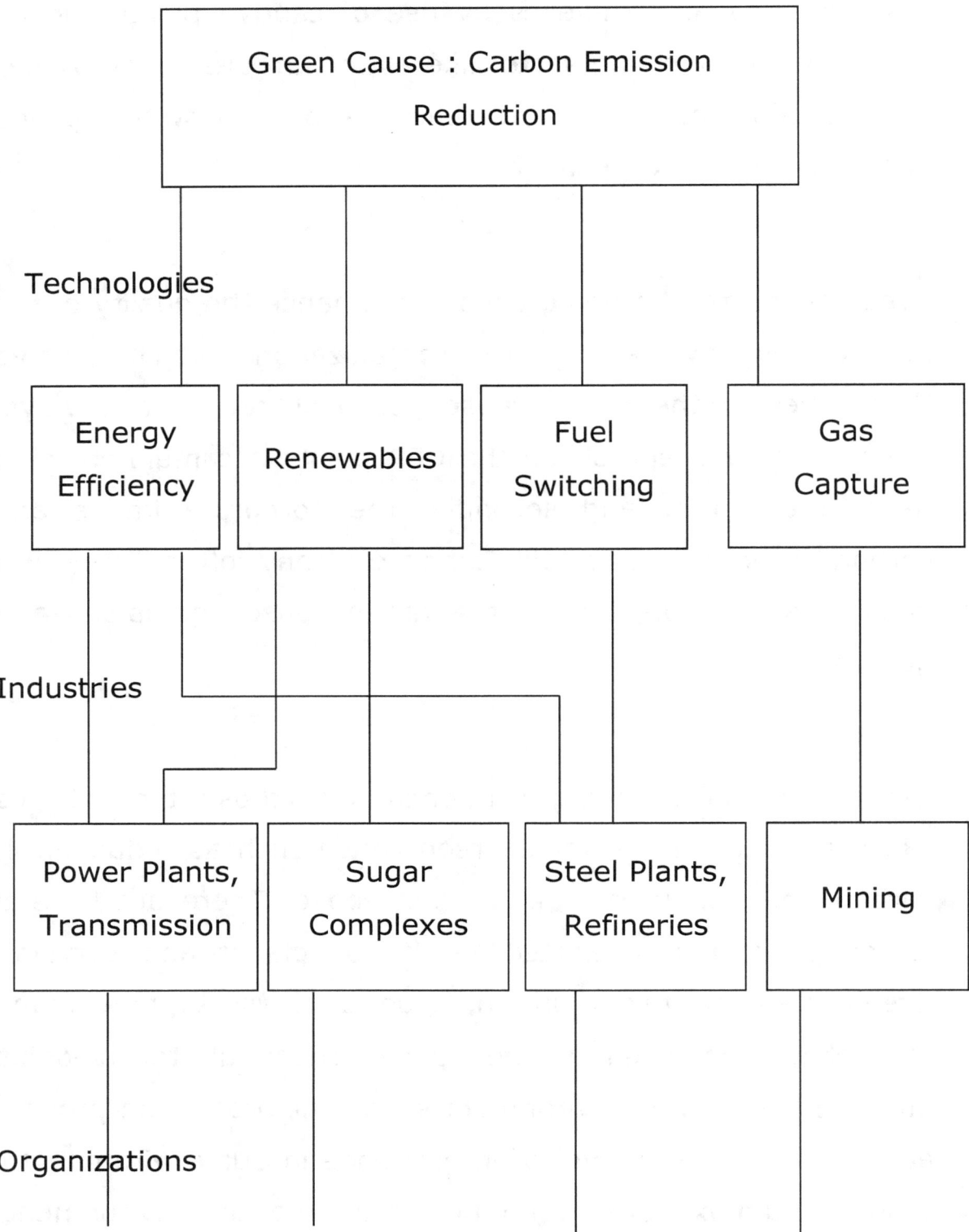

Hierarchy in Levels of Branding

Branding at a level has an impact on other levels. For Example, efforts at corporate level branding has a cascading impact on the product brands of the corporate also. The corporate brands act as an umbrella for the underlying product brands. Therefore, in promotion of a product brand, some efforts and resources may be redirected or shared towards the corporate brand building process.

Furthermore, from the four levels of branding discussed in previous sections, branding at three levels appear to have some cascading effect at some other levels also, which prompts an enquiry in finding a hierarchical relationship among them. The significance of understanding the hierarchy in the levels of branding is that, it allows to perceive which level act as umbrella for other level and how to share resources in the branding exercise.

The Product level branding is basic level and it is the lowest level at which Branding can be done. It does not act as umbrella for any other level of branding. Thus product level branding is lowest in hierarchy and it is targeted towards a single product or products in a single product class.

1. Corporate Brand Hierarchy

Corporate level branding acts as umbrella for various product level brands of the corporate and group companies. Some corporate brands are focused and are present in single product segment with few strong Brands.

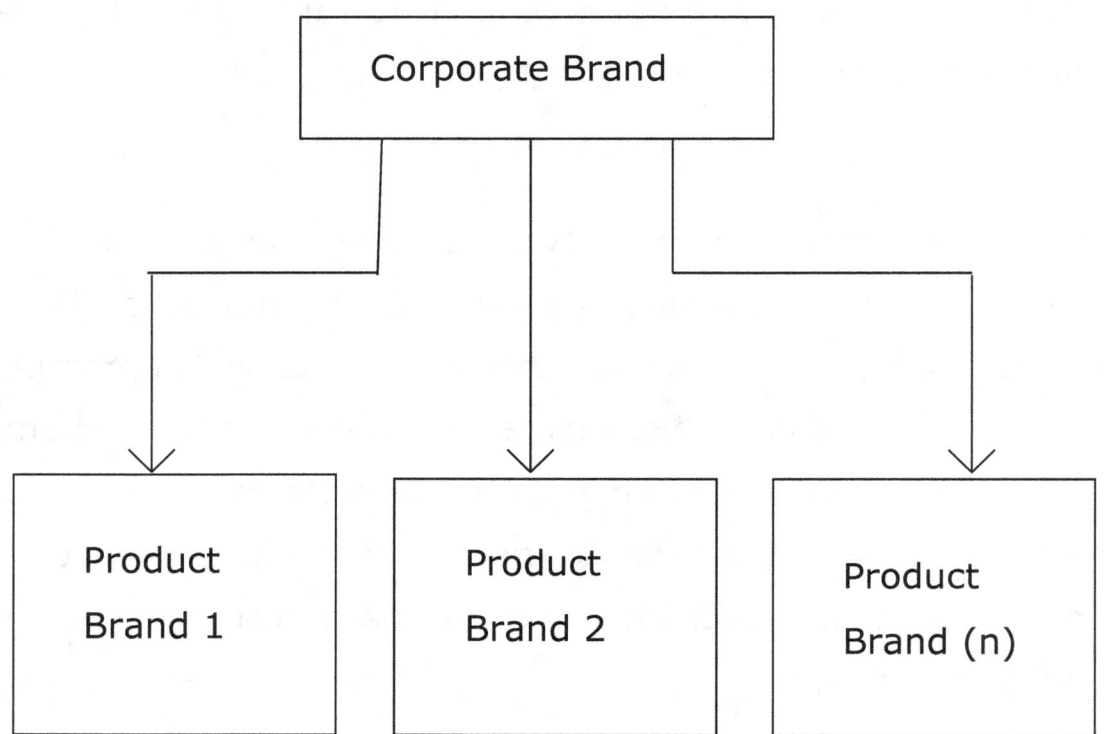

The above chart is also applicable for relatively smaller business groups with few manufacturing facilities and countable number of products and brands.

Spectrum of Branding Strategy

The strength, equity, versatility and acceptability of the corporate brand will have direct effect on the equity of the product brands of the corporate.

Colgate is focused company mainly in dental care and it later diversified in shaving segment also. It is a fit case for first type of corporate Brand, which are focused corporate with interest in one or countable few product segments.

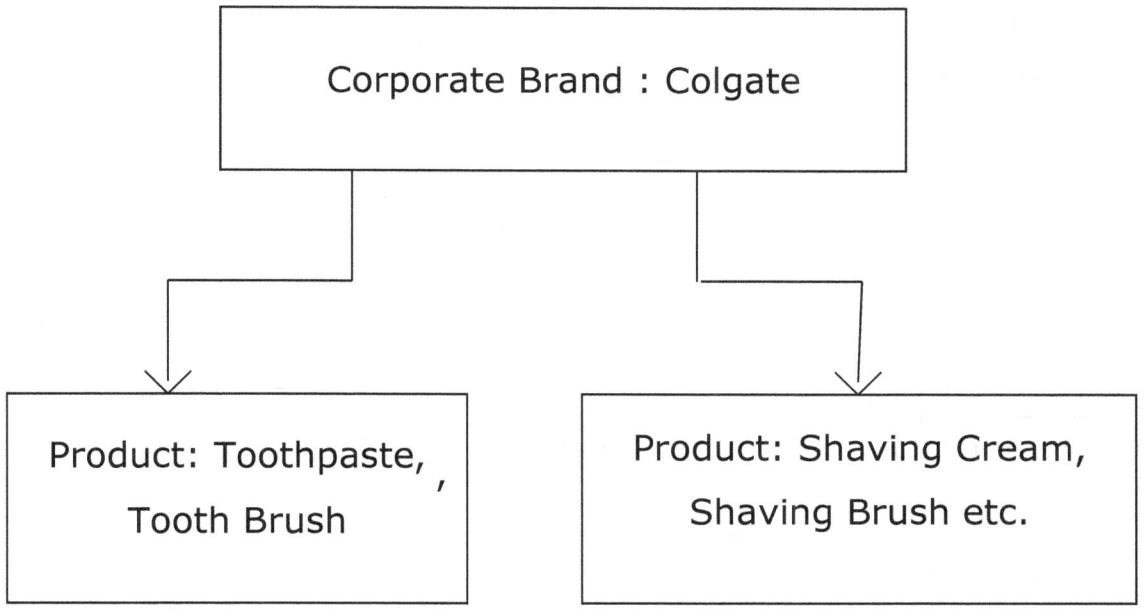

Thus Colgate may be considered as a brand which is focused in dental care and other personal care such as shaving. Only with countable few products the brand is known world-wide.

Micro Branding Strategies

Some corporate are largely diversified with presence in several sectors of business activity having many products to sell in each sectors.

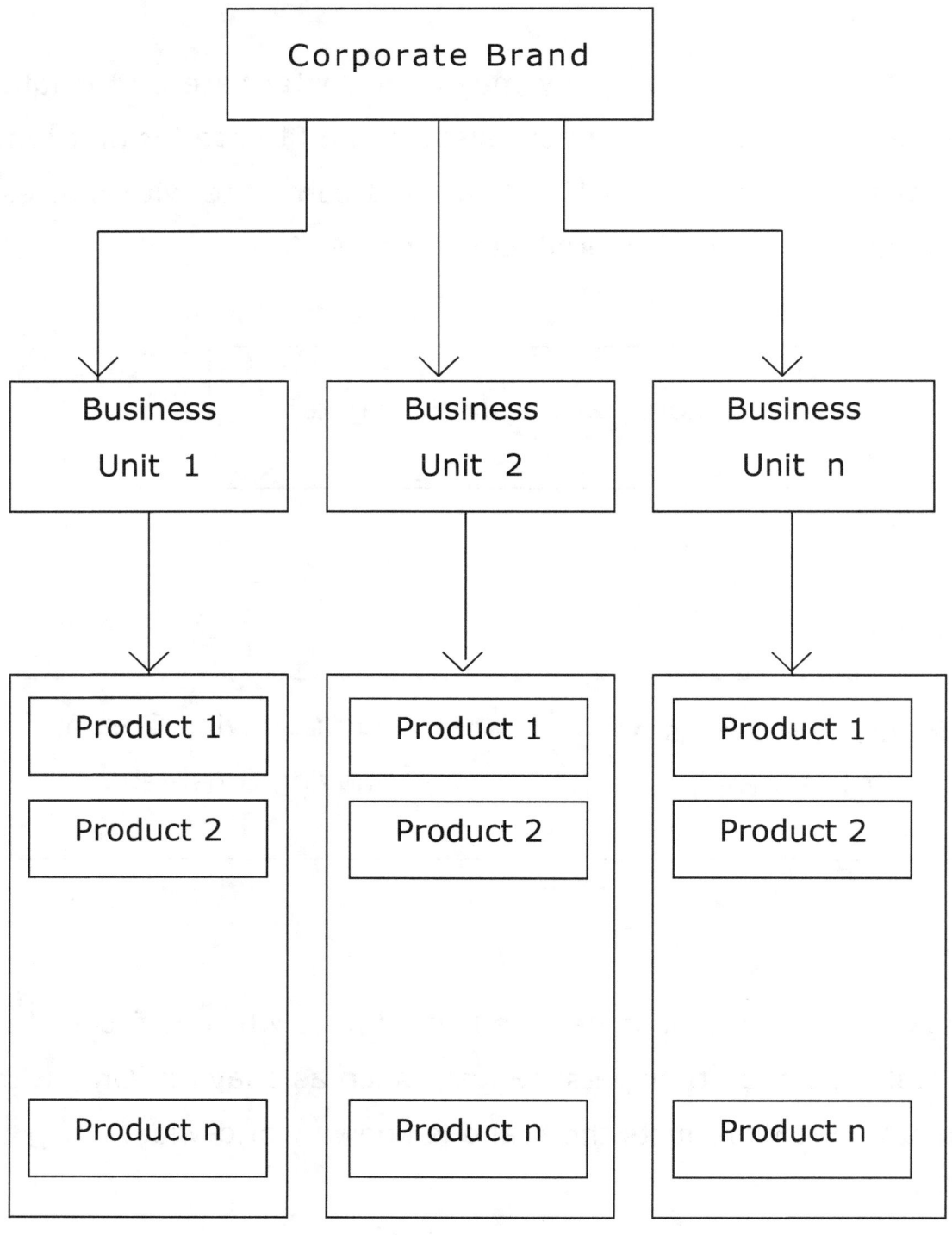

Spectrum of Branding Strategy

The previous flow chart shows the corporate brands hierarchy applicable for large business groups, which are present in diversified sectors of industry with several manufacturing plants and a number of products and brands.

An example of this phenomenon is TATA corporate brand. From the very beginning of the industrialization of India, TATA'S have been able to create a very much reliable corporate brand and the name TATA is virtually known to every citizen, literate and illiterate. It is also known for exhibiting quality and reliability in its products.

This has given them an opportunity to diversify in practically every sphere of business and the TATA products have been accepted vehemently by public within no time, whether it was tata tea, tata salt or tata indica car.

Starting with tisco (tata iron and steel) in steel and iron mining sector, tata name as corporate was established. Later other business units such as telco, tata chemicals, tata tea, tata sponge, tata consultancy, trent and tata elexi to name a few, were brought under ambit of the corporate brand tata. The products from these business units list from automobiles, chemicals and fertilizers, tea and coffee, computer software and hardware to retail and branded jewelry.

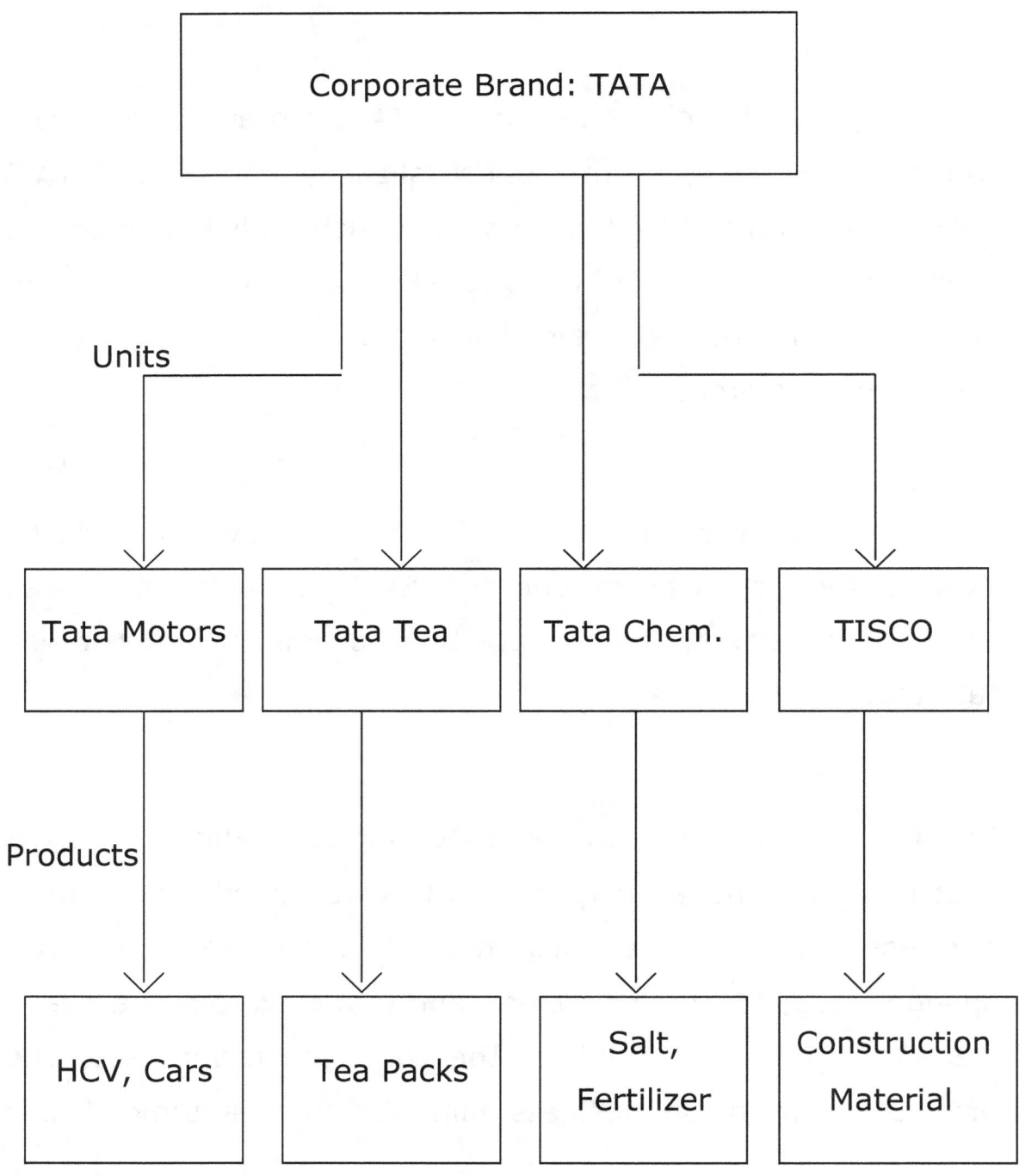

2. Technology Brand Hierarchy

Technology branding is phenomenon, which occurs when a new technology is replacing the existing technology or an invention has taken place, effecting a paradigm shift in the way business is done. Internet enabled personal computers or multimedia personal computers are example of replacing products and lap tops loaded with mobile chips are an inventive product.

The users addicted to graphics replace their ordinary personal computers with multimedia computers which are optimized for graphics applications. But laptops are not a replacement of personal computers, but it is an innovative product, which creates and satisfy a new need, that is a personal computer when one is in travel.

Technology branding acts as umbrella over corporate brands and products brands owned by corporate. When a new technology is being compared and seen better than existing technology, it is natural that products designed and operating on new technology gets promoted. The corporate , which join the new technology earliest are the gainers over their rivals. The new technology reaches the consumer through visionary corporate, which recognize new age technology before time.

The flow chart of technology branding hierarchy is shown in the diagram below

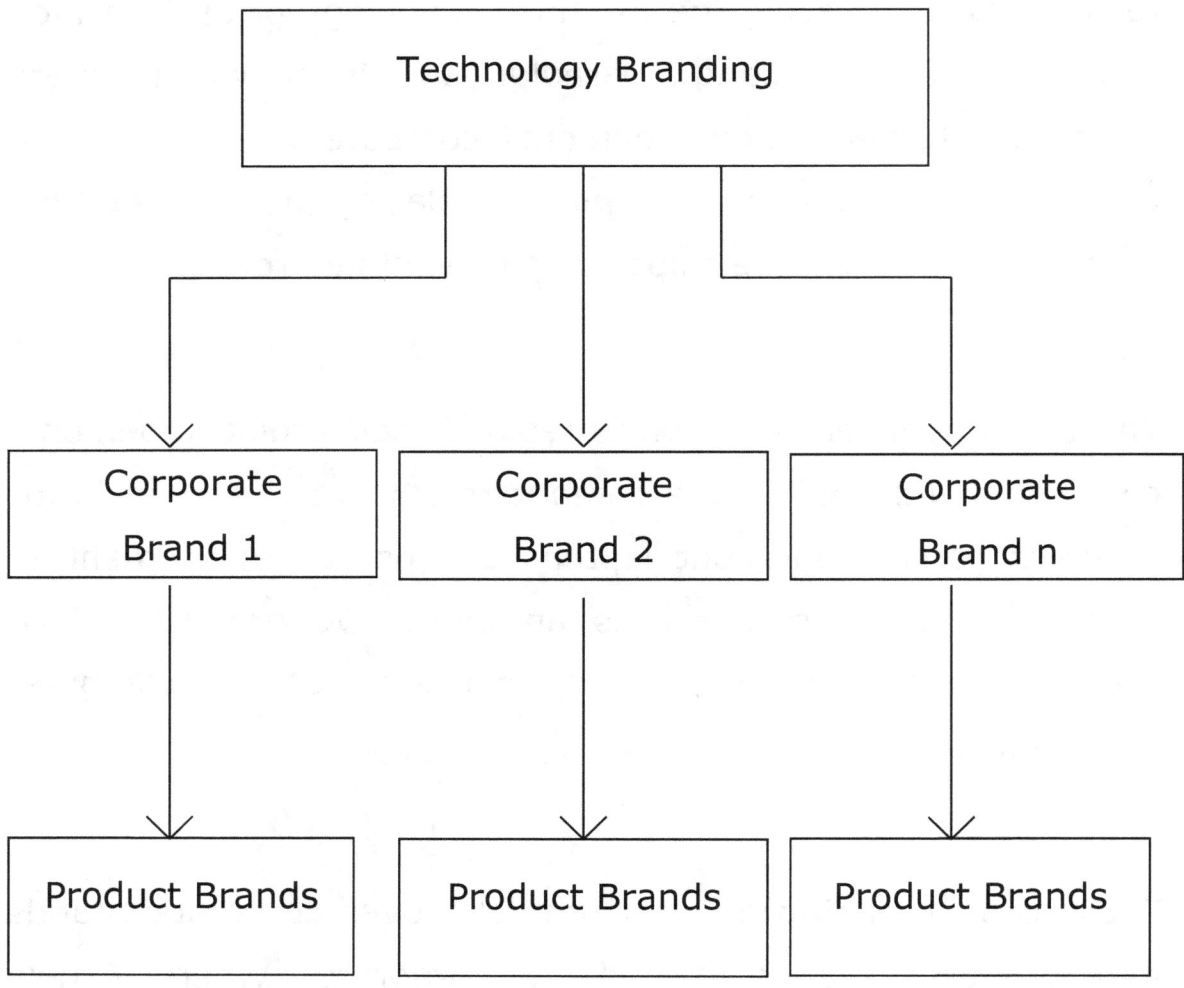

No sooner a new technology like internet was invented, it was adopted in many products, for example, in the Personal computers, Mobile handsets etc. They were promoted not by a single chip maker, a single personal computer manufacturer or

Spectrum of Branding Strategy

a single mobile handset manufacturer, rather all the major chip makers, all the major PC manufacturers and all the major mobile handset manufacturer started a campaign in unison about advantages of internet technology. Basically it was phenomenon of technology branding of internet technology.

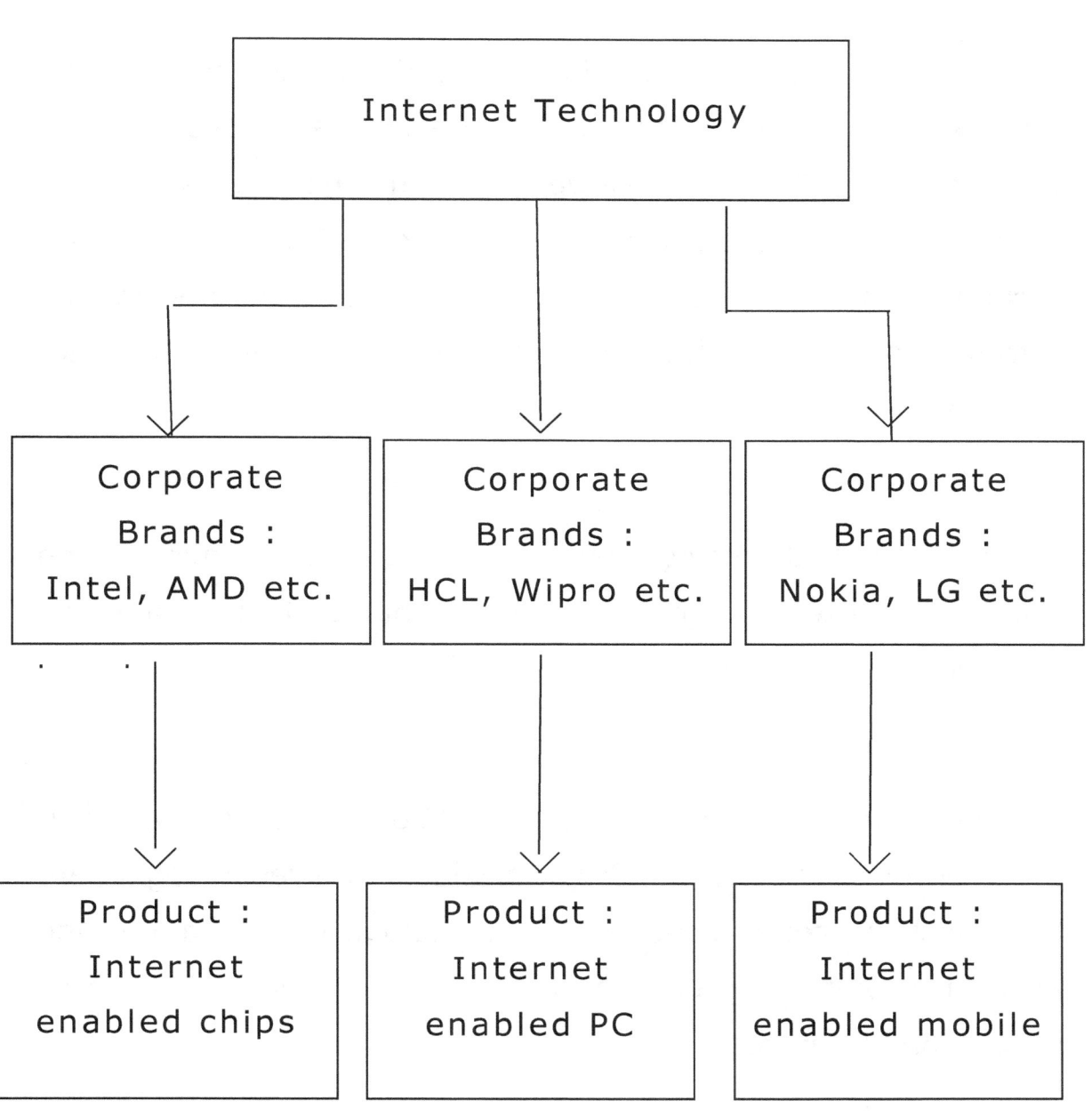

3. Green Brand Hierarchy

Not all technologies are nature friendly, rather most of the modern technologies pollute our environment and ecological system.

Domestic refrigerators running on CFC technology are one example of technologies, which pollute and destroy our environment. CFC based refrigerators emit materials which are responsible for destroying ozone layer. There are other technologies, which use different type of coolants in the refrigeration cycle, which does not emit unfriendly materials and are thus environment friendly.

When many technologies are emanating, the winner will no doubt be the technology which protect our earth and helps us keeping our environment green.

Societal marketing is the newest evolution in marketing, which focus on our society first. Green products and technologies are the most welcome concept in technological innovation and product design. A great concern is being given to towards protection of nature.

Green branding starts with an objective, which is invariably an environmental cause such as protection of ozone layer or reduce emission of gases causing green house effect etc. The objective can be achieved by several evolving technologies in different sphere of manufacturing involving many existing manufacturers. The green branding hierarchy is shown by a flow chart as under,

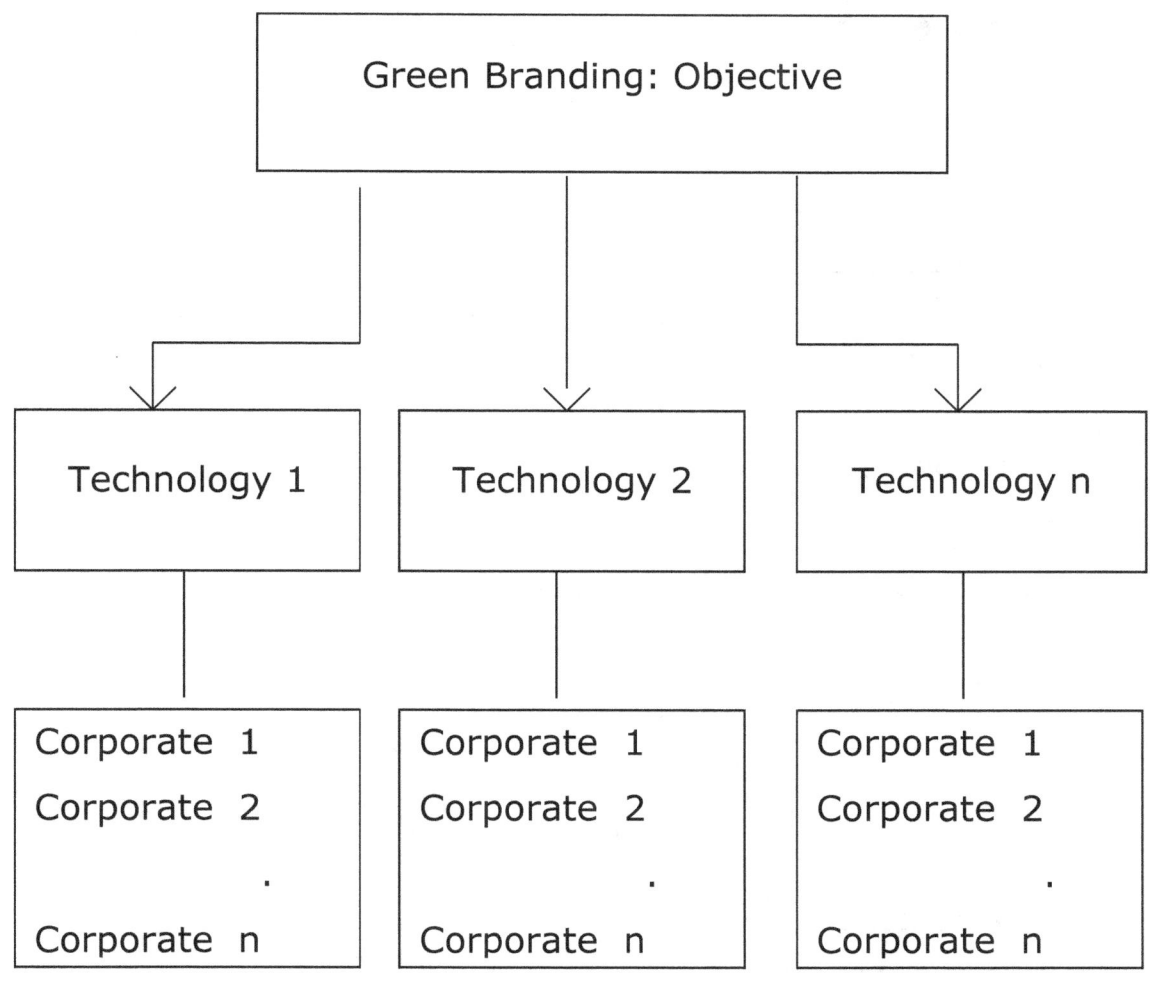

Micro Branding Strategies

Let us understand green branding hierarchy with an example.

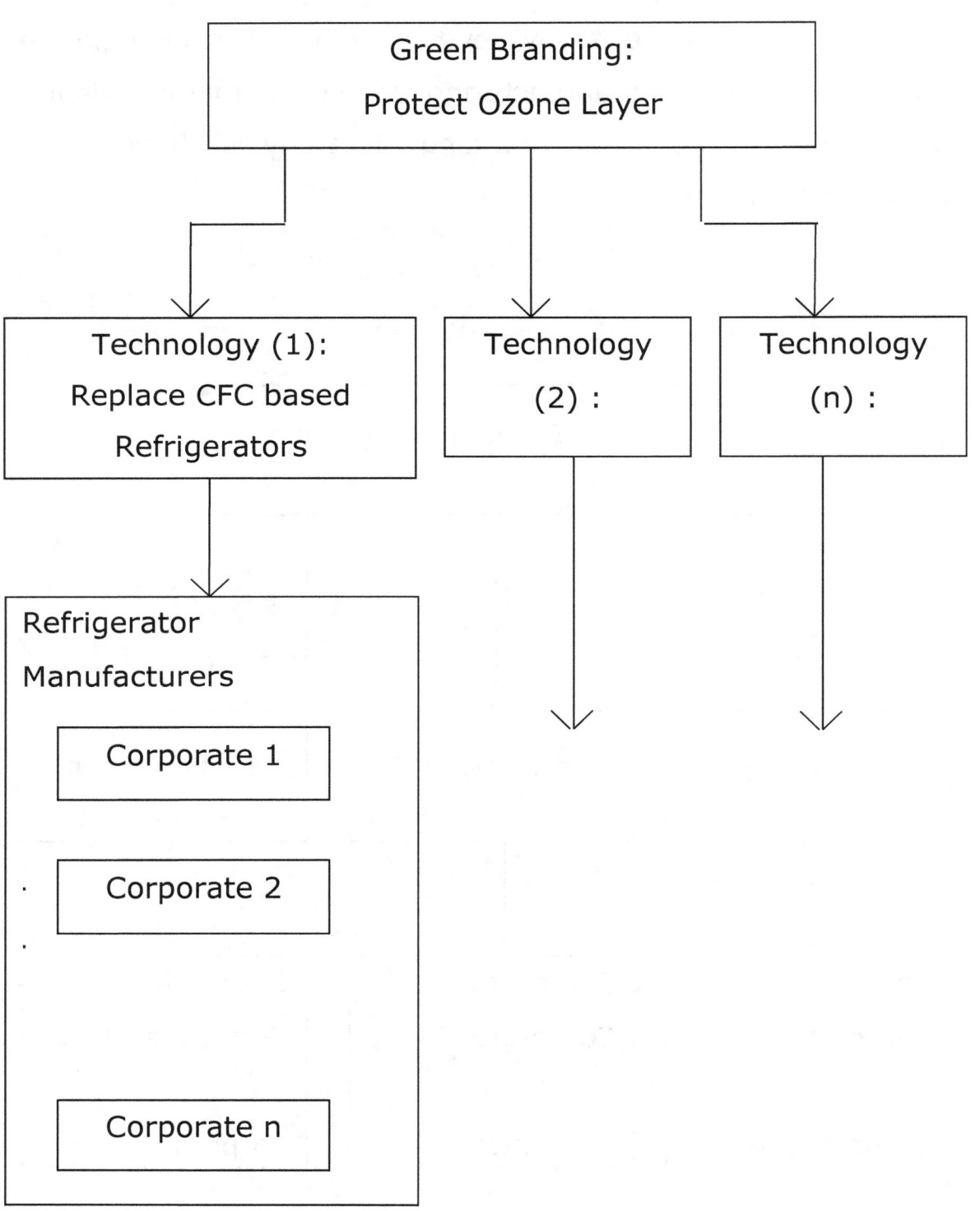

There are technologies, which contribute to the destruction of ozone layer at one hand and other new equivalent technologies, which does not destroy ozone layer. Green branding is about promoting those technologies which does not destroy ozone layer or our environment.

One reason for depletion of ozone layer is emission of CFC gases, which are used in domestic refrigerators by several manufacturing corporate. There are technologies for refrigeration, which do not use CFC gases and thus do not detriment the ozone layer. These environmentally friendly technologies must be adopted by corporate involved in refrigerator manufacturing. Thus under green cause "Protect ozone layer", CFC free refrigeration is one technology being promoted. Similarly if other reasons are known for depletion of ozone layer, the replacing technologies will also come under the same green cause. Similar is case of green cause of "reducing emission of green house gases". Emission of gases like carbon di oxide, carbon mono oxide, sulfur di oxide etc. are responsible for green house effect that results in global warming. Many technologies are available to reduce or eliminate the emission of these gases across industries like automobile and thermal power plants. These technologies are getting encouragement from all corners under the same green cause of reducing green house gases.

Significance of Levels of Branding

The understanding of these various levels of branding will help an organization in concentrating at various objects to be promoted as brand.

A deep understanding of various levels of branding will help an organization in

1. Rationally divide the total media efforts in effective way to promote product level brands and corporate as a brand.

2. When to start corporate level branding and promote diversified product brands under it.

3. When to promote a technology brand or join the promotion of a new technology in harmony with other innovators.

4. Creating a consortium to promote a new technology brand.

5. Promoting those green technologies which protect our environment, ecology and planet.

6. Exploiting the economic opportunities from people affection of green technologies and need being felt by the world towards a safer planet to live.

7. Understanding the proper brand architecture.

Brand Architecture Possibilities

Brand architecture is integral part of branding strategy. Four levels of branding has been found and a hierarchical relation among these levels has been established in previous discussions. At least three brand architectures emerge, in the light of these facts. These three brand architectures are

1. Corporate – Product Brand Architecture

2. Technology – Corporate – Product Brand Architecture

3. Green Cause – Technology – Corporate – Product Brand Architecture

1. Corporate – Product Brand Architecture

The simplest brand architecture is corporate and product brand architecture. Branding strategy in this architecture is affected by status of product brand in relation to the corporate brand. The relation between product and corporate is governed by how the target audience binds the product's identity with the corporate identity.

2. Technology – Corporate – Product Architecture

The next complexity in brand architecture is the common technology which is guiding the corporate and products both. In this configuration, An innovative technology may be promoted by consortium of several corporate.

3. Green Cause – Technology – Corporate – Product Brand Architecture

The ultimate goal of an enterprise should be to safe guard our planet and continuity of human survival. A green initiative may involve several technologies which improve many products, which were detrimental to environment otherwise. Important fact is that any green initiative is strongly supported by international bodies and governments. Branding strategy of a corporate must benefit it, from these bodies which support green cause.

Spectrum of Branding Strategy

Part 4

Branding Matrix Analysis

A brand must be analyzed to understand brand's presence and strength in order to maintain it's present status and brand equity in the market or to fortify it above present level. By understanding the segments where the brand is present substantially, we also come to know the segments, where it is not present. This could open new opportunities for the brand extension.

Let us assume that a brand is targeted for global reach. The brand has two variants, one with high technologies to offer high quality products and the other with standard technology to offer standard quality products. Thus we have two basic class of products under the brand. First one, is high quality products class with global reach and second is, standard quality products class with global reach. Each class can be examined to reveal in which of the income groups and age groups, the brand has made its impact in market. The exercise can be accomplished with help of a two dimensional matrix.

Case 1. Geographic Reach : Global

       Quality level   : High

Relevant income groups in the context of brand, are middle class, rich class and super rich class. The relevant age groups are youngsters, middle age and seniors. A two dimensional matrix can be designed to find out presence of the brand with age and income as two dimensions and tick marked.

Income \ Age	Young	Mid age	Seniors
Middle		√	
Rich	√	√	√
Super rich	√	√	

The above matrix highlights that the brand has made a position among youngsters of rich and super rich class, among mid age people of all the income groups and among seniors of rich group. It is obvious that youngsters of middle income group and seniors of middle income group and super rich class are not well aware of the brand. These could be niche market segments for brand spread.

Case 2. Geographic Reach : Global

Quality level : Standard

Relevant income groups are middle class and rich class. The super rich class is not attracted to the standard quality product class probably, they are interested in high quality products class only. The relevant age groups are youngsters, middle age and seniors. A two dimensional matrix can be designed with age and income as two dimensions, to find out presence of the brand and tick marked as in earlier case.

Age Income	Young	Mid age	Seniors
Middle	√	√	√
Rich		√	
Super rich		√	

The above matrix highlights that the brand has made a position among youngsters of middle income group only, among mid age people of all the income groups and among seniors of middle income group. It is obvious that youngsters and seniors of rich and super rich class are not well aware of the brand. These could be opportune market segments for brand spread.

If the products are consumed by both the genders, further gender based analysis must be carried out to find gender specific presence and strength of the brand. The following matrix is constructed with age and gender as two dimensions, to understand the gender orientation of the brand.

Gender \ Age	Young	Mid age	Seniors
Male	√	√	
Female		√	√

The information gathered highlight that the brand has a position in youngsters and mid age group of males and mid to senior age group of females. This also implies that youngster females and senior males are less aware of brand, which could be market segment where brand manager must pay attention. The matrix survey conveys two conclusions. First, brand has fortified in some segment, but is still weak in many segments. If brand was intended for unmarked segments also, it must chalk a strategy to strengthen its position in those segments. Second, the brand may not be having product variant for the unmarked segment at all. Say, for example there is no product to attract children or females in the brand line. This gives an opportunity to the brand for product line extension.

One more way of creating difference from competing brands is offering traditional knowledge such as herbal products in cosmetics and pharmaceuticals segments. The herbal products are not only part of environmentalism but come with assurance of no side effects, which modern scientific chemical based products do not guarantee. Value based branding is another way to brand one's product differently. In this case of branding organization must associate itself with a social value or cause, to attract people who believe in same value or cause. Thus uniqueness in brand can be created from these several strategies and edge over the competing brands can be attained in the market.

Next stage of understanding brand presence, involves knowing if brand was intended for novel cause. The brand might had differentiated itself from competitors on ground that, it stand for a social value, for example child care, gender equality, environmentalism, green technology or combination of more than one of these. If brand had any such intension, this must be verified that people and target market have received this hidden intention in the brand. If brand initially had no such cause to pursue and it is finding tough competition, it may opt to bundle itself with one or more social cause in itself to edge over other competing brands.

Let us take case of three brands competing with each other in a market. Brand1 created difference with introducing traditionalized variant of the brand. Brand2 and Brand3 too, opts for going with traditionalized products, little later. The next difference is created by Brand1 by introducing clean technology products and environment friendly corporate branding. This exercise puts Brand1 far ahead of other two brands in market. The Brand2 had no choice but to imitate brand1 and come with clean technology products, which reduce pollution. Brand3 remains lagging behind Brand2 in absence of any such initiative.

Since Brand1 has a green cause associated with it, the acceptability of Brand1 might still improve by becoming part of green branding cartel.

Matrix analysis can be applied in the above case too, having unique feature and brands as two dimensions of the matrix. The emerged matrix is drawn as below

Unique Feature	Traditionalized	Clean Technology	Environment Friendly
Brand1	√	√	√
Brand2	√	√	
Brand3	√		

Thus a brand should be analyzed and further strategy should be drawn by the organization to fortify existing brands or to create a new brand.

The niche areas identified may be fortified by a suitable macro branding strategy, micro branding strategy or brand repositioning, subject to intelligence and constrains of the organization.

Spectrum of Branding Strategy

Part 5

Glossary

Glossary

Brand

Brand is legally protected personality (in form of name, term, sign, symbol, design or combination of them) that represents a product, service, organization or any other entity and how the product, service, organization or the entity relates to people and customer.

Brand Management

Brand management is about application of sound principles in creating and maintaining a brand. Brand management involves creativity as well, and therefore it is an art also.

Brand Equity

Brand equity is brand's worth which is measured in totality and not just money value. Higher brand equity symbolizes greater customer satisfaction, customer loyalty and less price sensitivity.

Brand Valuation

Brand valuation is management technique to assign a value to brand in money terms. Brand is classified as intangible asset in accounting

Glossary

Brand experience

Brand experience is sensation, feeling or emotion evoked in a person by brand's action.

Brand Orientation

Brand orientation is orientation of whole organization towards brand in response to feedback or new information from market.

Brand Loyalty

Brand loyalty is tendency of a customer to purchase a brand repeatedly, unaffected by attracting actions of competitor brands.

Brand Awareness

Brand awareness is ability of a customer to recognize or recall a brand. Brand awareness is key parameter in purchase decision. Brand recall is supposed to be higher level of awareness compared to brand recognition.

Brand Extension

Brand Extension is market stretching exercise of an organization where organization uses same brand name to expand operations in different product category possibly because, the organization feels that its brand has reached a high level brand equity. A non success in brand extension may result into phenomena called brand dilution.

Brand Dilution

Brand Dilution is process in which a brand loses its previous strengths in the market. The weakening may result due to multiple use of brand, misjudgment in pricing or extended use of brands in different category of products.

Brand Repositioning

A brand is intended or positioned for specific market segment. Over time and experience, brand might stagnate in competition. To overcome stagnation and to distance the brand from competing other brands, organization may decide to reposition the brand by changing marketing mix i.e. product, price, promotion and place. Repositioning may also be in response to technological advancement.

www.ingramcontent.com/pod-product-compliance
Lightning Source LLC
Chambersburg PA
CBHW082331220526
45470CB00008B/2472